carry me

20 BOUTIQUE BAGS to SEW

YUKA **KOSHIZEN**

TABI NO HAJIMARI WA KONO BAG DE
Copyright ©2005 Yuka Koshizen

English language translation & production by World Book Media, LLC
For international rights inquires, email info@worldbookmedia.com

Originally published in Japanese language by SHUFU TO SEIKATSU SHA.
English translation rights arranged with SHUFU TO SEIKATSU SHA, Tokyo
Through Timo Associates, Inc., Tokyo.

First published in North America in 2009 by:

 INTERWEAVE.
interweavestore.com
201 East Fourth Street
Loveland, CO 80537-5655 USA

Printed in Singapore

Library of Congress Cataloging-in-Publication Data
Koshizen, Yuka.
Carry me : 20 boutique bags to sew / Yuka Koshizen.
p. cm.
ISBN 978-1-59668-184-2 (pbk.)
1. Handbags. 2. Tote bags. 3. Sewing. I. Title.
TT667.K68 2009
646.48—dc22
2009015721

10 9 8 7 6 5 4 3 2 1

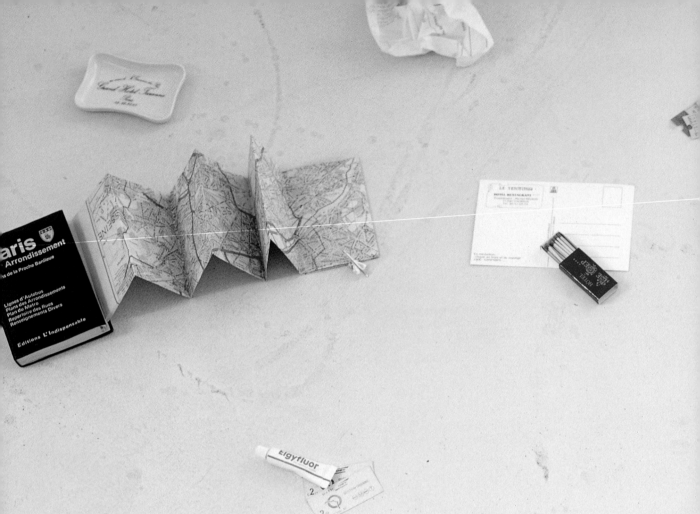

THE COLLECTIONS

Techniques and Instructions

#01　Winter Tweed Boston Bag and Small Purse
wool tweed + Indian silk

ウールツイード×インドシルク
アルミ口枠入りのボストンバッグ＋サブバッグ

Instructions on page 50

#02 Antique Print Tote/Shoulder Bag and Change Purse
blue, brown + white floral-print cotton

ヴィンテージコットンプリント×こげ茶のカツラギ
深さが変わる2wayトートバッグ＋口金ポーチ

Instructions on page 56

#03 Wayfarer Denim Tote and Zippered Clutch
dark blue vintage denim + striped cotton lining + eyelets + hardware

ヴィンテージデニム×コットンストライプ
ハトメとナスカン使いの大バッグ＋小バッグ

Instructions on page 62

#04 Duty-Free Expandable Carry-All and Pouch
raw white silk + snap hardware

帯芯×銘仙
バネホック使いの2wayトートバッグ＋ポーチ

Instructions on page 68

#05 Left Bank Granny Bag and Drawstring Day Bag
nautical-striped linen + red twill

麻のモノトーン変わりストライプ×赤のチノクロス
グラニーバッグ＋信玄袋

Instructions on page 74

#06 Business Class Laptop Bag and Circle Pochette

hickory-striped cotton + lime green cotton

ヒッコリーストライブ×黄緑色のコットン
縦横パッチワークのボストンバッグ＋ポシェット

Instructions on page 80

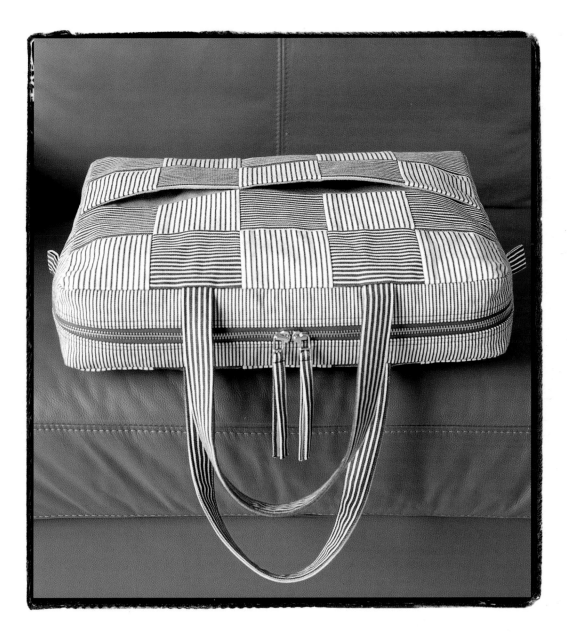

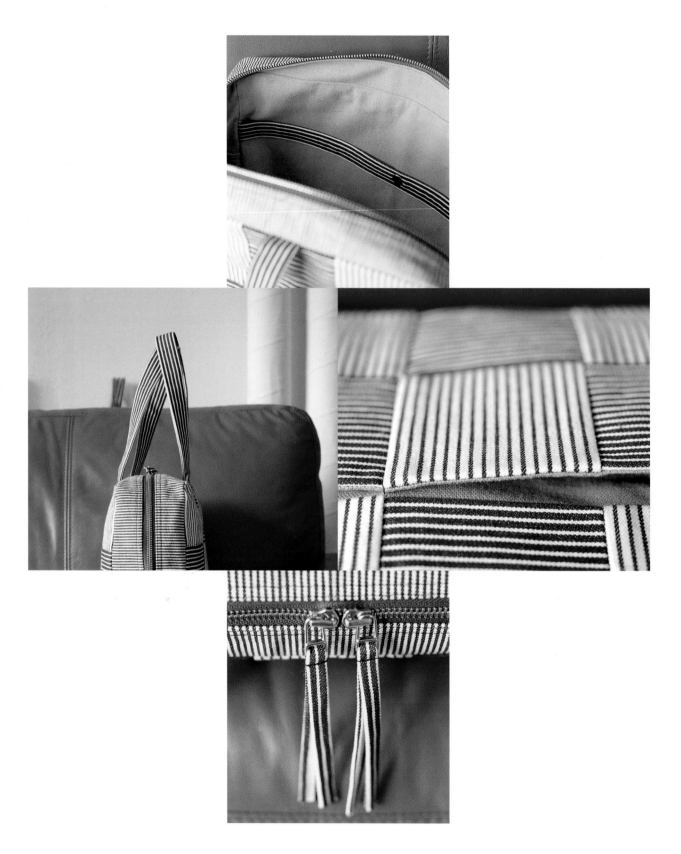

CARRY ME ⬟ *COLLECTION #06*

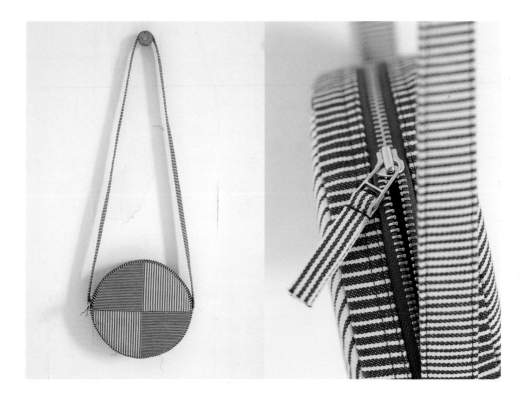

#07 Cabana Tote and Book Cover
multicolor striped canvas + black canvas

マルチストライプ×黒の帆布×方眼入りの帆布
小かぶせつきトートバッグ＋ブックカバー

Instructions on page 88

#08 Sidecar Messenger Bag and Corsage Rosette
plum flannel + vintage rayon print trim

フラノ×ヴィンテージレーヨンプリント
メッセンジャーバッグ＋コサージュ

Instructions on page 92

#09 Market Day Canvas Tote, Azuma Bag, and Furoshiki Wrapping Cloth
natural linen + cotton print + azuma wrapping cloth

麻帆布×手ぬぐい
トートバッグ＋東袋＋風呂敷

Instructions on page 98

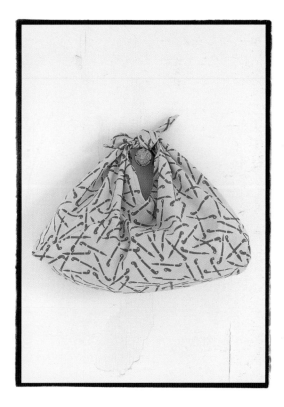

#10   Urban Travel Trunk and Luggage Tag
coated canvas + camouflage vinyl + eyelet straps

防水帆布×カムフラージュプリント
トランク型バッグ＋ネームタグ

Instructions on page 104

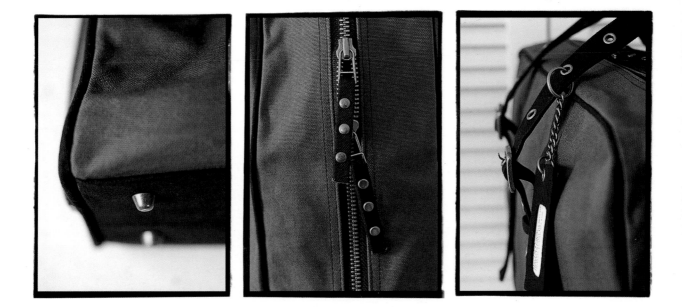

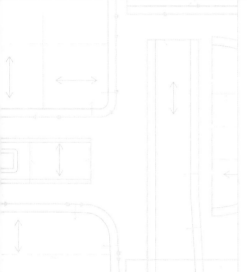

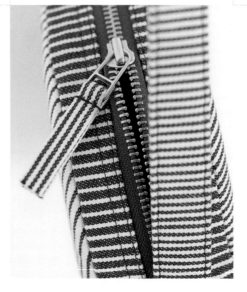

HOW TO MAKE

INSTRUCTIONS

Bag-Making Basics

🛍 Dimensions

The finished dimensions of each bag are given as *width × height × depth.* Measurements are given in inches (") and centimeters (cm) or millimeters (mm).

🛍 Bag Parts

The following figures illustrate the basic parts of three common bag styles. These names are used throughout the book. The largest part of a bag is the *main body* (or *front and back main bodies* when the front and back sides have different designs). The length of fabric (or distance) between the two panels of the main body is the *side*. Bags may have a number of different closures, including a *flap cover, small flap cover,* or a *tab closure*. When the main body and side pieces are sewn together it is called an *outer bag* or a *lining bag*.

🛍 About the Patterns

In this book, full-size patterns are provided on the pull-out pattern sheet for pieces with curves or non-rectangular shapes. Pieces with straight edges are illustrated in diagrams. One bag's components may be given in both patterns and drawings. The instruction pages indicate whether full-size pattern pieces are provided on the pattern sheet.

🛍 How to Choose Fabrics

This book mainly uses natural fiber fabrics, such as cotton, linen, and wool. Due to the relatively large bag sizes, fabrics with tight or durable weaves work best. Feel free to experiment with fabrics, but avoid delicate fabrics or stretch fabrics, which may eventually cause the bag to lose its shape.

🛍 Choosing and Using Interfacings

For these bags, interfacings are used for various purposes, such as affixing to outer and/or lining fabrics or inserting between the bottom fabrics. Select them according to the fabric and design for your bag. For inside pockets, shoulder straps, and handles, the interfacing should be cut to fit the piece without seam allowances. For all other bag pieces, cut to fit the entire surface of each fabric piece including the seam allowance.

🛍 Fusible Interfacings

Most of the pattern pieces in this book will be interfaced. Lightweight fusible interfacings are easy to apply, are widely available in many types and weights, and are suitable for bag main bodies, pockets, and handles. Interfacing is generally sold in 18" (45 cm) width. To interface pattern pieces larger than 18" (45 cm), two pieces of interfacing can be abutted side by side (make sure all fabric is covered).

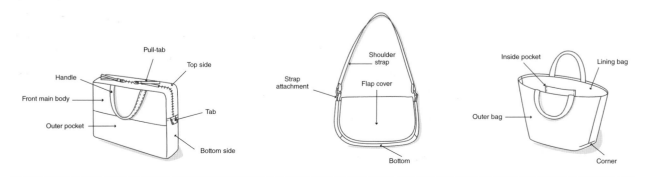

To fuse interfacing, follow manufacturer's instructions for iron settings. Place adhesive side of interfacing against wrong side of fabric. Beginning in the middle and working out, hold the iron in place for about 10 seconds; never slide the iron. Lift the iron and place it on another position, then repeat until the entire interfacing surface is bonded to the fabric. Let cool. Remember: The adhesive (fusible) side of the interfacing should face the wrong side of the fabric.

Heavyweight Interfacings

Heavyweight interfacings are used to stabilize the bottom of some of the bags and areas of fabric where metal fittings, such as grommets and rivets, are attached. Some types are made with a self-adhesive side, with a sheet of peel-away paper protecting a layer of glue. Remove the release paper to affix the self-adhesive side of the interfacing to the wrong side of the fabric. Heavyweight fusible interfacings are also available.

If you prefer, sew-in heavyweight interfacings can also be used. Small pieces of heavyweight interfacing are used to stabilize an area where metal parts are to be attached. Cut a piece of interfacing slightly larger than the metal part and adhere or fuse to the wrong side of the fabric.

Using Fabric Selvages and Weave Texture in Design

Some bags in this book incorporate the original lengthwise fabric edge, called the selvage, in the design. These edges are tightly woven and will not fray. Traditional Japanese kimono fabric is about 14" (35 cm) in width, sometimes making it possible to use both selvages. Thus, some bag pieces will be cut so the weave is oriented with the lengthwise grain of the fabric. Long, narrow bag pieces, such as shoulder straps, are best created this way, allowing the fab-

ric to be used more efficiently than cutting widthwise. To ensure stability, apply a fusible interfacing to the wrong side of the strap fabric, as noted above.

Marking Fabric Pieces

The goal of marking pieces is to precisely determine the center line of symmetry. If the main body openings and bottoms, pockets, and handle attachment positions are symmetrical, they will not lead to serious construction or design issues, even if the top-to-bottom (vertical) dimensions are slightly off. (It is always better if everything is accurate, of course.) As soon as a piece is cut out, find and mark the center line. In addition, mark any pocket and handle attachment positions, side opening bottoms, and for curved pieces, alignment points. Use chalk, fabric pencils or markers, or snip notches (V-shaped cuts) in the seam allowance.

Using Fabric Glue

Traditionally, fabrics are temporarily held together with pins or thread basting before final stitching. Fabric glue can also be used. Look for clear-drying glue marked for use with fabric and use a spatula or wooden craft stick to apply to seam allowances. These adhesives are useful in many situations, including when sewing together slippery fabrics, holding pockets in place, keeping seam allowances flat, and preventing raw fabric edges from fraying. Always wait for the glue to dry before sewing the fabric and use a press cloth when pressing over glued areas to protect your iron. Also, do not glue the fabrics too securely if the seam allowances are to be pressed flat after sewing. Be careful not to allow any of the adhesive to peek or seep through to the right side of the fabric.

📌 Sewing Tips

- Read through all directions, review all diagrams carefully, and try to envision the entire construction process before you begin. Capital letters in the text instructions refer to the diagrams on the following pages.

- Find the pattern pieces on the full-size pattern sheet for the bag you plan to make. Trace pattern pieces onto tracing paper, pattern paper, or any lightweight paper (you can tape the pattern sheet to a window and then place your tracing paper over it to see the lines easily, if needed). Cut out the traced pattern pieces and pin to fabric, noting if any edges should be placed on the fold of fabric. Double arrows indicate the grainline and should be placed on grain of fabric (parallel to the selvage).

- For pattern pieces without a full-size pattern, cut to the measurements shown in the diagram. Instructions may be written near the diagram telling you what to cut; for example, "2 fabric, 2 lining, 2 interfacing" means "cut two pieces of the main fabric to the indicated measurements, two pieces of lining fabric to these measurements, and two pieces of interfacing to these measurements."

- Fuse interfacing pieces to wrong side of fabric following manufacturer's instructions. Interfacing may be narrower than fabric width; if necessary for large pieces, cut interfacing in strips to fit fabric and butt edges of interfacing pieces against each other as you fuse so the entire piece of fabric is interfaced.

- A ⅜" (1 cm) seam allowance is included on full-size patterns in this book unless indicated. Cut fabric on the bold outside line or to the measurements shown in diagram if no pattern piece is given. Sew seams ⅜" (1 cm) from the outside edge. If you prefer, mark the ⅜" (1 cm) seam line at the same time that you trace the pattern.

- For a lined bag, sew the lining just slightly smaller than the outer bag (1–2 mm). It's easy to just increase the seam allowance slightly. Similarly, when sewing the lining and outer bag together to assemble the bag, set in the lining about ¼" to ⅜" (0.5–1 cm) for a clean finish. Nest the lining inside the outer bag before sewing along the top opening.

- Set your sewing machine for a medium length stitch, about 8 stitches to the inch (2.5 cm). Backstitch at the beginning and end of a line of sewing, especially at openings for turning pieces right side out, bottoms of side seams, pockets, or wherever there will be more stress on the stitching. Backstitching reinforces the seam and prevents the thread from raveling easily.

- When sewing a simple curved seam, you can sew the straight sections first and then sew the curved portion to form the complete seam, as shown in the illustration below:

🛍 Finishing Seam Allowances

Seam allowances are ⅜" (1 cm) on the full-size patterns, but a narrower seam allowance is used on some small bag parts. For a neat finish, trim seams after sewing to ¼" (6 mm) and remove bulk from corners and curved seams. To do this, cut diagonally across the seam allowance at corners, as shown in illustration, being careful not to cut stitching. After turning right side out, use a point turner or other blunt-point object to gently push the corner out. On curved seams, clip into the seam at several places, being careful not to cut all the way through stitching. Press after turning right side out. Shaping your seam allowances carefully will help create a beautiful bag.

🛍 About Metal Notions and Other Hardware

In this book, many types of metal hardware are used; some require tools such as hammers and pliers. Some, such as grommets, rivets and spring hooks, require size-specific tools. Read manufacturer's instructions (or consult with the store's staff) when buying tools. For making holes, sewing tools such as grommet hole punchers and a buttonhole chisel may be used as well. Zippers are listed in the materials lists in the exact lengths needed. If necessary, buy a longer zipper and shorten it by taking several hand-stitches with heavy thread across the zipper teeth to create a new zipper stop at the length desired, or simply tuck the extra zipper length beneath the bottom of the bag's side opening after inserting.

🛍 Pressing

Ironing is not just for smoothing out wrinkles before cutting the fabric; you should iron, or press, frequently as you sew. Press seam allowances open or to one side after stitching each seam or bag section and press the finished bag to ensure a smooth, refined finish. (Hint: This final pressing will help camouflage small flaws in the seams.)

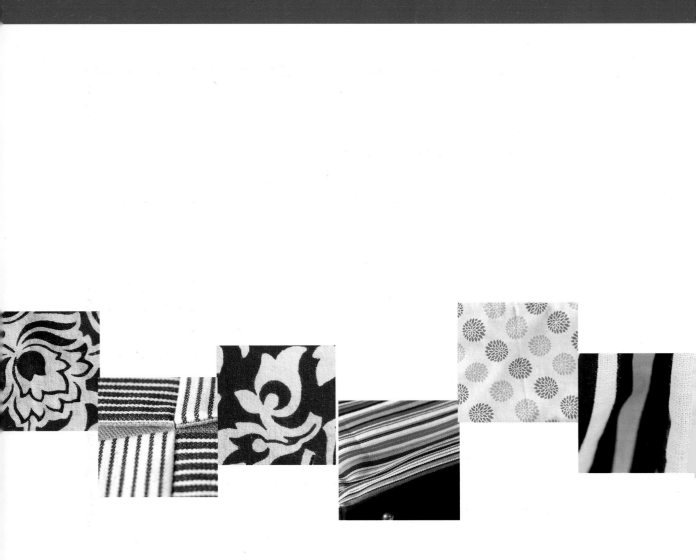

🛍 Inspired Fabrics

When planning to sew a bag, I rarely buy all new materials. I like to combine fabrics from my stash with ones that I newly acquire. That way, I have to use my imagination. Sometimes I bring fabric (or swatches) to the store when shopping for coordinating fabrics. Delicately patterned vintage fabrics especially benefit from being held side by side with new patterns.

"Meeting" a fabric is fate. If you pass by a fabric without buying it, it may be gone forever, even the ones that seem simple or common. You should purchase at least half a yard (about 18" [50 cm]) of a fabric you fall in love with, even when you have no idea what to use it for. These fabrics will inspire you to create later down the road.

While traveling, I cherish these fateful encounters. Sometimes I fall in love with a fabric's motif, sometimes the feel of it in my hand, or the texture of its weave. My interest is further piqued, and I feel a thrill when I realize that it may be a once-in-a-lifetime fabric opportunity. I may not come here again—so I'll seize the moment!

I have accumulated quite a stash of fabrics over time. Looking at each of them, I remember each trip, each occasion, on which I acquired it. This nostalgia makes it hard for me to put scissors to it. Remember, they are better off being sewn with than collecting dust (however prettily). If they are sewn into a favorite bag, they can stay even closer to you, and you can enjoy it more often.

Some of my personal favorite fabrics turned into the pieces shown in this book. Some had been in my stash for several years. Acquiring fabrics while traveling, stitching them into bags at home, then traveling again with the new bag—a perfectly inspired life cycle.

Winter Tweed Boston Bag and Small Purse
COLLECTION #01

The Winter Tweed Boston Bag and Small Purse are surprisingly simple to construct, though they look professionally finished. With the metal bag frame for structure and the leather handles as accents, these bags are trim and polished—a touch of elegance for your travel ensemble.

About the Fabric
Choose wool tweed for the outer bag fabric; look for something with a nubby weave that would make a wonderful winter coat. For the lining, choose a silk with a luxurious feel and sheen, such as douppioni silk (sometimes called Indian silk).

Winter Tweed Boston Bag
15" wide × 13¾" high × 4¾" deep (38 × 35 × 12 cm)

Small Purse
9¾" wide × 4¾" high × 2" deep (25.5 × 12 × 5 cm)

Materials
Wool tweed (outer fabric): 36" × 44" (91.5 × 112 cm)
Indian or douppioni silk (linings and inside pocket fabric): 36" × 40" (90 × 100 cm)
Lightweight fusible interfacing (for lining and inside pocket fabric): 18" × 72"
    (45 × 180 cm)
Medium-weight fusible interfacing (for outer bag fabric): 18" × 68" (45 × 170 cm)
Heavyweight fusible interfacing (for bag bottoms/gussets): 8" × 4" (20 × 10 cm)
Stabilizing foam interfacing, such as Clover Shape n Create Bag/Tote Foam Stabilizer
    (for bottom of Winter Tweed Boston Bag): 15" × 4¾" (38 × 12 cm)
Leather straps:
    One ⅝" (1.5 cm) wide and 79" (200 cm) long (for straps on Winter Tweed Boston Bag
    and Small Purse)
    One ¾" (2 cm) wide and 4" (10 cm) long (for Small Purse tab)
Wooden rings (6): ¾" (2 cm) diameter
Double-sided rivets (12): ¼" (6 mm) diameter
Purse feet (4, for Winter Tweed Boston Bag): ⅝" (1.5 cm) diameter
Base for fabric-covered buttons (1, for Small Purse): ½" (1.3 cm) diameter
Aluminum bag frame, hinged (1, for Winter Tweed Boston Bag): 12" × 4" (30.5 × 10 cm)
Fabric glue
Grommet hole puncher
Rivet setting tools

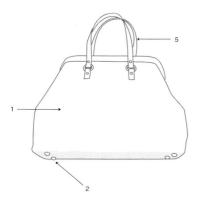

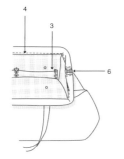

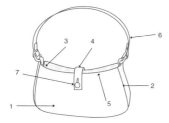

Winter Tweed Boston Bag

1. Fuse lightweight interfacing to the wrong side of lining bag and inside pocket pieces and medium-weight fusible interfacing to the wrong side of the outer, lining, and inside pocket fabric pieces.

2. Fuse heavyweight interfacing to the wrong side of the outer fabric where the rivets will be inserted. Affix the stabilizing foam interfacing onto the wrong side of the bottom fabric. Attach the purse feet. Sew side seams to bottom of side opening and sew bottom corners widthwise (A).

3. Create the inside pocket and sew it to the lining fabric (B). Sew together the sides and the bottom/corners of lining.

4. Insert the lining bag (3) into the outer bag (2). Sew side openings as shown. For each of the two top opening parts, fold down three times and sew (C).

5. Pass each end of the leather straps through their respective rings to create the two handles. Attach the handles to the bag using the rivets (D).

6. Pass the bag frame pieces through the trifolded top seam. Attach the frame pieces (E).

Small Purse

1. Fuse medium-weight interfacing to the wrong side of all the outer bag pieces and lightweight interfacing to lining bag fabric pieces.

2. Fuse heavyweight interfacing to the bottom part of the bottom/gusset outer fabric. Sew bottom/gusset to the two main body outer fabric pieces (A).

3. Leaving an opening for turning right side out, sew together the main body lining and bottom/gusset lining fabric pieces.

4. Create a buttonhole in the leather tab (for closing the bag). Temporarily baste the tab to the outer bag (B).

5. Insert the lining bag inside the outer bag (B) and sew around the top opening (C). Turn right side out and blind-stitch the opening closed.

6. Create and attach the fabric-covered button.

#01 WINTER TWEED BOSTON BAG AND SMALL PURSE

Use Side A for full-size sewing pattern for Winter Tweed Boston Bag and Small Purse main body and bottom. Measure and cut out the following pieces directly on the fabric (no pattern provided):

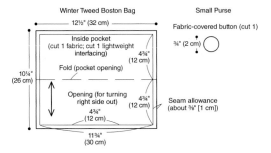

Winter Tweed Boston Bag

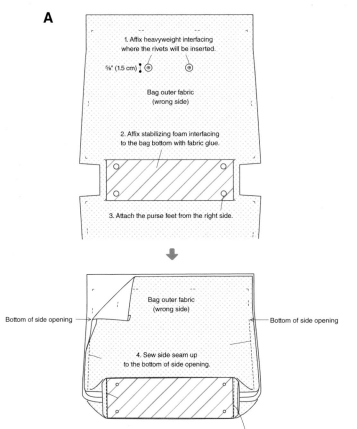

B

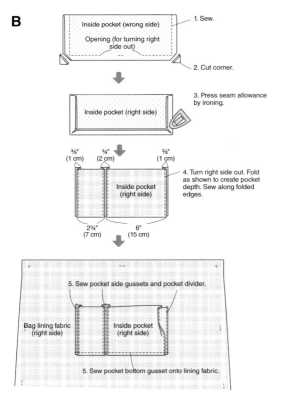

Inside pocket (wrong side)

1. Sew.

Opening (for turning right side out)

2. Cut corner.

3. Press seam allowance by ironing.

Inside pocket (right side)

³⁄₈" (1 cm)　³⁄₄" (2 cm)　³⁄₈" (1 cm)

Inside pocket (right side)

4. Turn right side out. Fold as shown to create pocket depth. Sew along folded edges.

2³⁄₄" (7 cm)　6" (15 cm)

5. Sew pocket side gussets and pocket divider.

Bag lining fabric (right side)

Inside pocket (right side)

5. Sew pocket bottom gusset onto lining fabric.

C

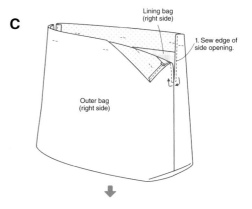

Lining bag (right side)

1. Sew edge of side opening.

Outer bag (right side)

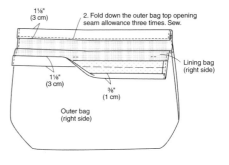

1¹⁄₈" (3 cm)

2. Fold down the outer bag top opening seam allowance three times. Sew.

1¹⁄₈" (3 cm)

³⁄₈" (1 cm)

Lining bag (right side)

Outer bag (right side)

#01 WINTER TWEED BOSTON BAG AND SMALL PURSE

D

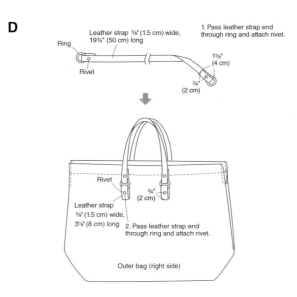

Ring

Leather strap ⅝" (1.5 cm) wide, 19¾" (50 cm) long

1. Pass leather strap end through ring and attach rivet.

Rivet

1⅝" (4 cm)

¾" (2 cm)

Rivet

¾" (2 cm)

Leather strap ⅝" (1.5 cm) wide, 3⅛" (8 cm) long

2. Pass leather strap end through ring and attach rivet.

Outer bag (right side)

E

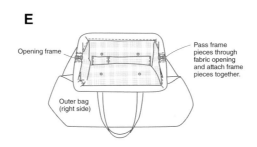

Opening frame

Pass frame pieces through fabric opening and attach frame pieces together.

Outer bag (right side)

Small Purse

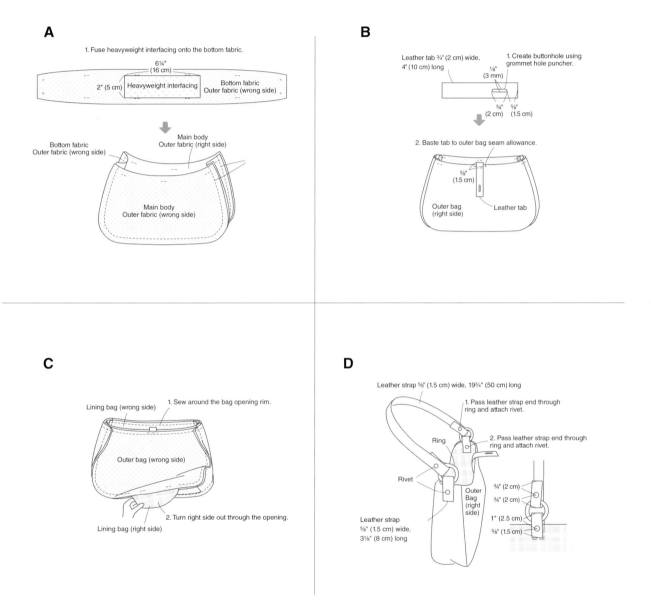

A

1. Fuse heavyweight interfacing onto the bottom fabric.

6¼"
(16 cm)

2" (5 cm) | Heavyweight interfacing

Bottom fabric
Outer fabric (wrong side)

Bottom fabric
Outer fabric (wrong side)

Main body
Outer fabric (right side)

Main body
Outer fabric (wrong side)

B

Leather tab ¾" (2 cm) wide,
4" (10 cm) long

1. Create buttonhole using
grommet hole puncher.

⅛"
(3 mm)

¾"   ⅝"
(2 cm) (1.5 cm)

2. Baste tab to outer bag seam allowance.

⅝"
(1.5 cm)

Outer bag
(right side)

Leather tab

C

Lining bag (wrong side)

1. Sew around the bag opening rim.

Outer bag (wrong side)

2. Turn right side out through the opening.

Lining bag (right side)

D

Leather strap ⅝" (1.5 cm) wide, 19¾" (50 cm) long

1. Pass leather strap end through
ring and attach rivet.

Ring

2. Pass leather strap end through
ring and attach rivet.

Rivet

Outer
Bag
(right
side)

¾" (2 cm)

¾" (2 cm)

1" (2.5 cm)

⅝" (1.5 cm)

Leather strap
⅝" (1.5 cm) wide,
3⅛" (8 cm) long

Antique Print Tote/Shoulder Bag and Change Purse
COLLECTION #02

This dual-purpose bag can be used as a tote or a shoulder bag, depending on your day's needs. Its shoulder strap can be worn crosswise, messenger style. The vintage cotton's blue-brown motif stands out in this simple design.

About the Fabric

This vintage cotton was acquired at a flea market in Paris. This small piece (only about one yard) had been biding its time in my sewing room for nearly ten years before it finally became a bag. It seemed to have been pre-washed a few times, making this cloth soft and easy to sew. The linings, trim, strap, and bottom of the Tote/Shoulder Bag are made from Katsuragi-style fabric, a medium-to-heavy cotton twill used for work clothes or uniforms.

Tote/Shoulder Bag

16¾" × 16¾" × 4¾" (40 × 40 × 12 cm)

Change Purse

7" × 5" (18 × 13 cm)

Materials

Cotton print fabric (Tote/Shoulder Bag outer bag fabric and Change Purse outer bag
    fabric): 36" × 28" (90 × 70 cm)
Katsuragi-style fabric or cotton twill (all other pieces): 36" × 44" (90 × 110 cm)
Lightweight fusible interfacing: 18" × 76" (45 × 193 cm)
Heavyweight fusible interfacing (for Tote/Shoulder Bag bottom): 11" × 4¾" (28 × 12 cm)
Hinged metal purse frame (1, for Change Purse): 5" × 2¼" (12.5 × 5.5 cm)
Twisted paper strip (for Change Purse): 20" (51 cm) long
Fabric glue

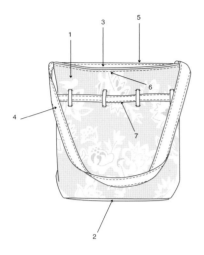

Tote/Shoulder Bag

1. Fuse lightweight interfacing to the wrong side of the main body outer fabric, bottom outer and lining fabrics, shoulder strap, band, and inside pocket fabric. Also fuse heavyweight interfacing to the wrong side of the bottom lining fabric.

2. Sew the side seam of the main body outer fabric, right side in. Sew to the bottom outer fabric (A).

3. Make the inside pocket and sew onto the main body lining fabric (B). Sew the side of the main body lining fabric right side in. Sew to the bottom lining fabric.

4. Make the shoulder strap and pin to the lining bag of Step 3 (C).

5. Insert the lining bag made in Step 4 into the outer bag of Step 2 and sew the top together. Leave a small opening for turning (D).

6. Turn the bag right side out from the small opening left in Step 5 and sew around the edge of the top opening. Make and sew the belt loops onto the bag (E).

7. Fold and press the band fabric. Pass it through the belt loops and sew it so it encircles the bag (F).

Change Purse

1. Fuse heavyweight interfacing to the wrong side of the outer bag fabric.

2. Sew the outer bag fabrics right side in along a U-shape line between the side opening bottoms (A). Sew the lining bag fabrics in the same manner.

3. Insert the lining bag into the outer bag and sew the top between the side opening bottoms. Leave a small opening on one side for turning (B).

4. Turn the purse right side out. Apply the fabric glue to the metal frame where the fabric will be inserted. Use an awl to push the fabric edges into the metal frame. Insert the long twisted paper and tighten the frames with pliers (C).

#02 ANTIQUE PRINT TOTE/SHOULDER BAG AND CHANGE PURSE

Use Side A for full-size sewing pattern (for Change Purse). For Tote/Shoulder Bag, cut out the following pieces directly from the fabric:

Tote/Shoulder Bag

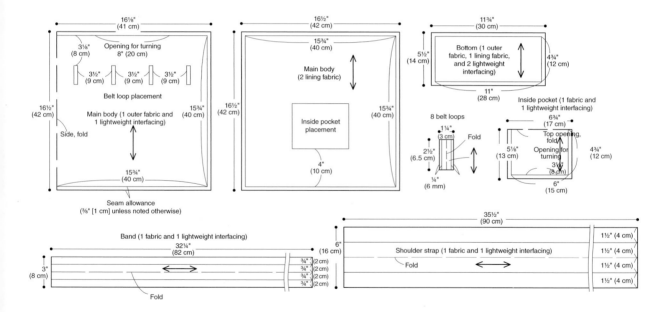

16⅛" (41 cm)

3⅛" (8 cm)

Opening for turning 8" (20 cm)

3½" (9 cm) 3½" (9 cm) 3½" (9 cm)

Belt loop placement

16½" (42 cm)

Side, fold

Main body (1 outer fabric and 1 lightweight interfacing)

15¾" (40 cm)

15¾" (40 cm)

Seam allowance (⅜" [1 cm] unless noted otherwise)

16½" (42 cm)

15¾" (40 cm)

Main body (2 lining fabric)

Inside pocket placement

15¾" (40 cm)

4" (10 cm)

11¾" (30 cm)

5½" (14 cm)

Bottom (1 outer fabric, 1 lining fabric, and 2 lightweight interfacing)

4¾" (12 cm)

11" (28 cm)

Inside pocket (1 fabric and 1 lightweight interfacing)

8 belt loops

1¼" (3 cm) Fold

2½" (6.5 cm)

¼" (6 mm)

6¾" (17 cm)

5⅛" (13 cm)

Top opening, fold

Opening for turning

3⅛" (8 cm)

6" (15 cm)

4¾" (12 cm)

Band (1 fabric and 1 lightweight interfacing)

32¼" (82 cm)

3" (8 cm)

Fold

¾" (2 cm)
¾" (2 cm)
¾" (2 cm)
¾" (2 cm)

35½" (90 cm)

6" (16 cm)

Shoulder strap (1 fabric and 1 lightweight interfacing)

Fold

1½" (4 cm)
1½" (4 cm)
1½" (4 cm)
1½" (4 cm)

Tote/Shoulder Bag

A

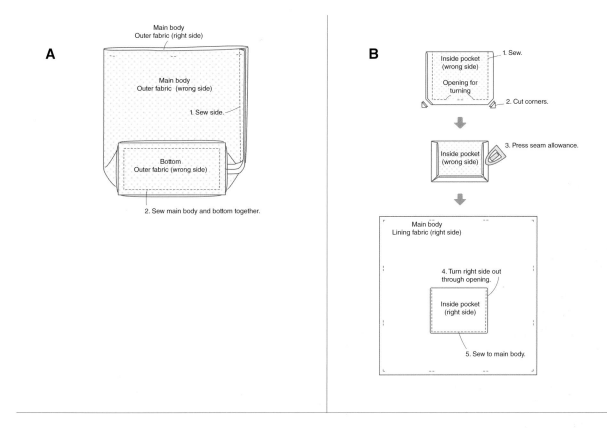

Main body
Outer fabric (right side)

Main body
Outer fabric (wrong side)

1. Sew side.

Bottom
Outer fabric (wrong side)

2. Sew main body and bottom together.

B

Inside pocket
(wrong side)

1. Sew.

Opening for
turning

2. Cut corners.

Inside pocket
(wrong side)

3. Press seam allowance.

Main body
Lining fabric (right side)

4. Turn right side out
through opening.

Inside pocket
(right side)

5. Sew to main body.

C

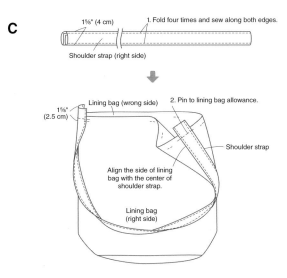

1⅝" (4 cm)

1. Fold four times and sew along both edges.

Shoulder strap (right side)

1⅝"
(2.5 cm)

Lining bag (wrong side)

2. Pin to lining bag allowance.

Shoulder strap

Align the side of lining
bag with the center of
shoulder strap.

Lining bag
(right side)

continued on next page ◉

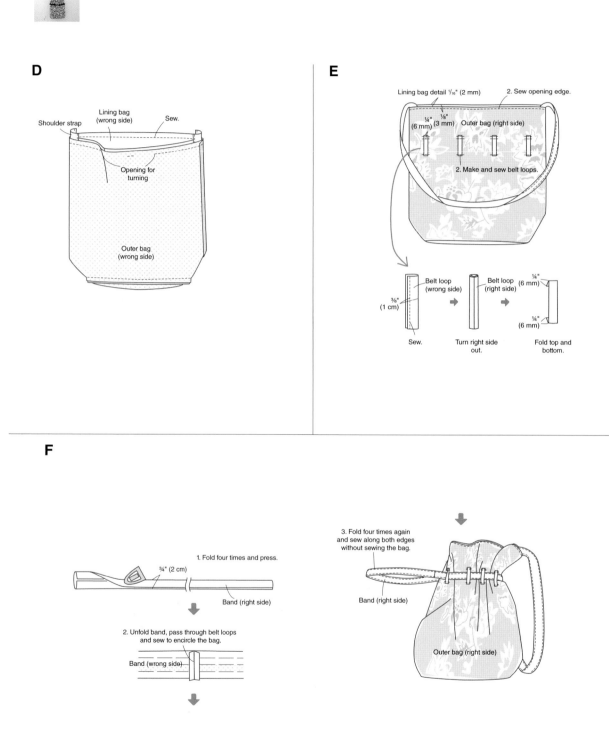

D

Shoulder strap

Lining bag (wrong side)

Sew.

Opening for turning

Outer bag (wrong side)

E

Lining bag detail ¹/₁₆" (2 mm)

2. Sew opening edge.

¼" (6 mm) ⅛" (3 mm) Outer bag (right side)

2. Make and sew belt loops.

Belt loop (wrong side)

Belt loop (right side)

¼" (6 mm)

⅜" (1 cm)

¼" (6 mm)

Sew.

Turn right side out.

Fold top and bottom.

F

1. Fold four times and press.

¾" (2 cm)

Band (right side)

2. Unfold band, pass through belt loops and sew to encircle the bag.

Band (wrong side)

3. Fold four times again and sew along both edges without sewing the bag.

Band (right side)

Outer bag (right side)

Change Purse

A

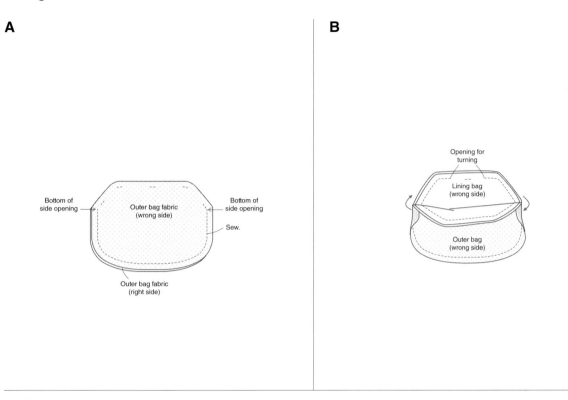

Bottom of side opening

Outer bag fabric (wrong side)

Bottom of side opening

Sew.

Outer bag fabric (right side)

B

Opening for turning

Lining bag (wrong side)

Outer bag (wrong side)

C

1. Apply fabric glue inside frame groove.

Fabric glue

Hinged metal frame for top opening

Awl

2. Insert bag opening edge into frame groove.

Outer bag (right side)

Strip of twisted paper

3. Insert twisted paper.

4. Tighten metal frame.

Press.

Outer bag (right side)

Pliers

Wayfarer Denim Tote and Zippered Clutch
COLLECTION #03

This bag features optional handles and a shoulder strap, which are interchangeable depending on the situations. The more wear and tear denim has endured, the more the weave loosens and the fabric stretches. Keep this in mind when placing the pattern pieces on used (or well-loved) fabric. Avoid cutting pattern pieces from denim jeans with thick seams. All seam allowances for the bag should be the same width.

About the Fabric

Denim gradually becomes weathered over time. In particular, note the whitened fabric around grommets and other metal details. Watch out for blue hands if the denim has never been washed!

Denim Tote

16½" × 13¾" (42 × 35 cm)

Zippered Clutch

9½" × 8" (24 × 20 cm)

Materials

Vintage denim (outer bag fabric and outer pocket, handles, and shoulder strap): 32" × 63" (80 × 160 cm)

Striped cotton (lining bag fabric, outer pocket lining, and inside pocket): 36" × 36" (90 × 90 cm)

Lightweight interfacing (woven fusible for lining bag fabric, outer pocket, and inside pocket): 18" × 63" (45 × 160 cm)

Zippers:

Wayfarer Denim Tote: 15¾" (40 cm)

Zippered Clutch: 8" (20 cm)

Double-sided grommets (16): #25, ¾" (18 mm) diameter

Swivel hooks (6): ¾" (20 mm)

Strap adjuster (1): ¾" (20 mm)

Double-sided rivets (6): ⁵⁄₁₆" (9 mm)

Grommet hole puncher

Rivet setting tool

Cutting the Denim
The bag and outer pocket pieces use the fabric side edge. The shoulder strap and handles are cut from the middle (as shown).

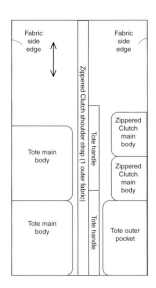

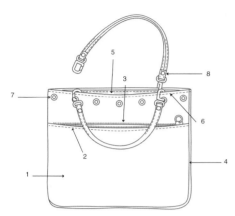

Denim Tote

1. Fuse lightweight interfacing to the wrong side of the lining fabric pieces for the bag, the outer pocket, and the fabric for the inside pocket.

2. Sew the outer and lining fabrics of the outer pocket right side out with the zipper inserted between (A).

3. Sew the remaining free side of zipper onto one of the outer bag fabrics, as shown (B). Fold the pocket fabric down right side out and pin the outer pocket edge onto the bag fabric (C).

4. Sew together the outer bag and outer pocket fabrics from one side to another across the bottom (C).

5. Make the inside pocket and sew onto one of the lining bag fabrics (see p. 59, B). Sew the two lining bag fabrics right side in from one side to another across the bottom.

6. Insert the lining bag into the outer bag and sew the top (D).

7. Insert the grommets as shown in photo.

8. Sew the handles, pass them through the swivel hooks (E), and set the rivets.

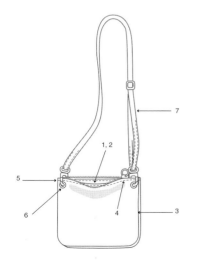

Zippered Clutch

1. Fuse lightweight interfacing to the back of the lining bag fabric.

2. Sew the two lining bag fabrics right side in from one side to another across the bottom.

3. Sew the zipper onto the outer bag fabrics and fold the bag fabrics right side in to sew from one side to another across the bottom (A).

4. Insert the lining bag of Step 2 into the outer bag of Step 3, open the zipper, and sew the top opening edge from the inside (B).

5. Close the zipper and sew both ends of the top from outside (C).

6. Insert the grommets as shown in photo.

7. Sew the shoulder strap, pass it through the swivel hooks and strap adjuster, and set the rivets (D).

#03 WAYFARER DENIM TOTE AND ZIPPERED CLUTCH

Use Side A for full-size sewing pattern (for Tote main body and outer pocket; and Zippered Clutch main body fabric).

Besides the above pattern pieces, cut out the following pieces directly from the fabric:

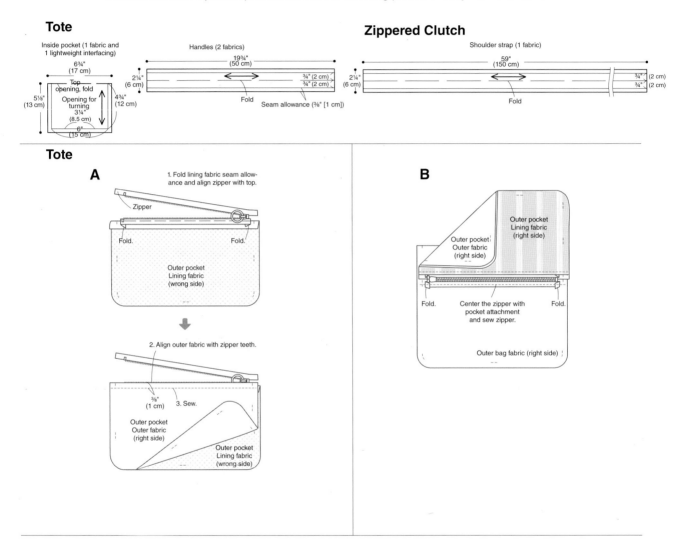

Tote

Inside pocket (1 fabric and 1 lightweight interfacing)

6¾" (17 cm)

Top opening, fold

5⅛" (13 cm)

Opening for turning 3¼" (8.5 cm)

4¾" (12 cm)

6" (15 cm)

Handles (2 fabrics)

19¾" (50 cm)

2¼" (6 cm)

¾" (2 cm)
¾" (2 cm)

Fold

Seam allowance (⅜" [1 cm])

Zippered Clutch

Shoulder strap (1 fabric)

59" (150 cm)

2¼" (6 cm)

¾" (2 cm)
¾" (2 cm)

Fold

Tote

A

1. Fold lining fabric seam allowance and align zipper with top.

Zipper

Fold.

Fold.

Outer pocket Lining fabric (wrong side)

2. Align outer fabric with zipper teeth.

⅜" (1 cm)

3. Sew.

Outer pocket Outer fabric (right side)

Outer pocket Lining fabric (wrong side)

B

Outer pocket Lining fabric (right side)

Outer pocket Outer fabric (right side)

Fold.

Center the zipper with pocket attachment and sew zipper.

Fold.

Outer bag fabric (right side)

C

Outer bag fabric (right side)

Outer pocket Outer fabric (right side)

Pin to bag fabric allowance.

D

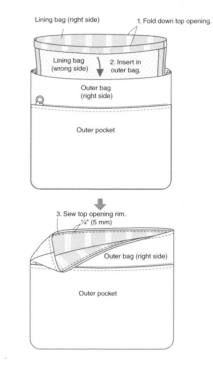

Lining bag (right side)

1. Fold down top opening.

Lining bag (wrong side)

2. Insert in outer bag.

Outer bag (right side)

Outer pocket

3. Sew top opening rim. ¼" (5 mm)

Outer bag (right side)

Outer pocket

E

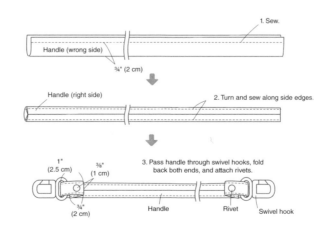

1. Sew.

Handle (wrong side)

¾" (2 cm)

Handle (right side)

2. Turn and sew along side edges.

1" (2.5 cm)   ⅜" (1 cm)

3. Pass handle through swivel hooks, fold back both ends, and attach rivets.

¾" (2 cm)

Handle   Rivet   Swivel hook

#03 WAYFARER DENIM TOTE AND ZIPPERED CLUTCH

Zippered Clutch

A

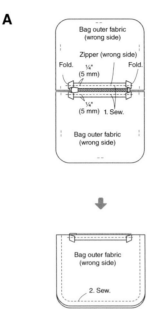

B

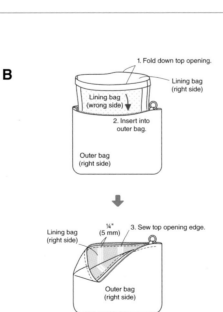

C

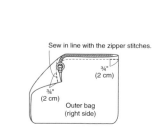

Sew in line with the zipper stitches.

¾"
(2 cm)

¾"
(2 cm)

Outer bag
(right side)

D

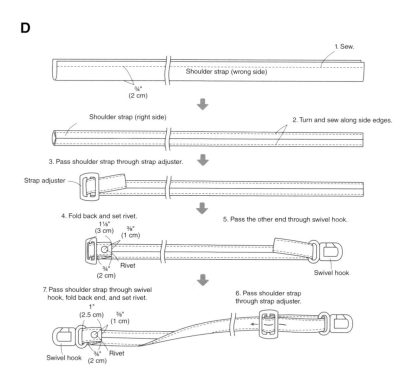

1. Sew.

Shoulder strap (wrong side)

¾"
(2 cm)

Shoulder strap (right side)

2. Turn and sew along side edges.

3. Pass shoulder strap through strap adjuster.

Strap adjuster

4. Fold back and set rivet.

1⅛"
(3 cm)

⅜"
(1 cm)

¾"
(2 cm)

Rivet

5. Pass the other end through swivel hook.

Swivel hook

7. Pass shoulder strap through swivel hook, fold back end, and set rivet.

1"
(2.5 cm)

⅜"
(1 cm)

Swivel hook

¾"
(2 cm)

Rivet

6. Pass shoulder strap through strap adjuster.

Duty-Free Expandable Carry-All and Pouch
COLLECTION #04

This tote spotlights authentic Japanese materials: Sanada braid for the handle and Meisen silk for the pocket. The elegant white, silver, and purple color combination is beautiful and modern. With as many as thirty-six cleverly placed snaps, its depth and width are expandable. The Pouch's main fabric was harvested from a kimono sash's lining.

About the Fabrics

The outer bag fabric is Obi-shin, a lining for kimono sashes traditionally made of a rough, somewhat stiff cotton fabric called Mikawa cotton; cotton duck or sailcloth can be substituted. The lining fabric is Meisen silk, a type of print kimono silk popular in Japan in the 1950s; any lovely silk print may be used, or look for vintage kimono fabric. Sanada braid is a flexible braided cotton tube once used by samurai warriors, and here it is filled with cotton cord. A sturdy braid found in the home decorating department can be substituted. Kamogawa thread is used for the optional decorative stitching; substitute cotton or rayon embroidery floss.

Duty-Free Expandable Carry-All

14¼" × 14¼" × 4¼" (snaps closed) × 11" (snaps open) (36 × 36 × 11 × 28 cm)

Pouch

9½" × 6¼" × 1⅝" (24 × 16 × 4 cm)

Materials

Kimono sash interfacing or cotton duck (outer bag fabric for Carry-All and Pouch and lining fabric for Carry-All inside pocket): 14¼" × 128" (36 × 325 cm)

Meisen silk or silk print fabric (outer fabric for Carry-All inside pocket, lining fabric for Pouch): 11¾" × 32" (30 × 80 cm)

Lightweight fusible interfacing (for lining fabric for Carry-All inside pocket and Pouch): 18" × 20" (45 × 50 cm)

Heavy-duty snaps (36 sets): ½" (13 mm)

Sanada braid or other braid: about ⅜" thick × 56" long (1 × 142 cm)

Cotton cording (if using Sanada braid): ¼" thick × 8¾ yds (5 mm × 8 m)

Kamogawa thread #18 or embroidery floss (optional)

Zipper (1, for Pouch): 8" (20 cm)

Decorative zipper pull (1, for Pouch)

Carry-All

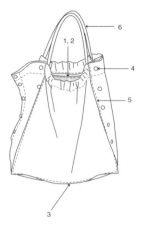

1. Fuse lightweight interfacing to the wrong side of the inside pocket outer fabric.

2. Make the inside pocket (A).

3. Layer the two bag fabrics in a cross shape. Sew around the center square sides to create the bag bottom. Insert the top side of the inside pocket into one of the bag top edges, which is folded down three times. Sew all top hems (B).

4. Fold and sew tucks along the entire side panel, as shown (C), and attach the heavy-duty snaps (C).

5. Sew the four sides to create the bag structure. Use the Kamogawa thread to handsew a running stitch. Sew only the outer two fabrics and leave the folded hem ends open to pass through the Sanada braid (D).

6. Pass six cotton ropes through the Sanada braid and pass it through the bag top hem. Sew the two ends of the braid together to form a circle (E).

Pouch

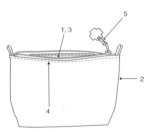

1. Fuse lightweight interfacing to the wrong side of the lining bag fabric.

2. Sew the zipper to the outer bag fabric and fold the bag right side in to sew the sides and bottom corners (A).

3. Sew the sides and bottom corners of the lining bag fabric.

4. Fold the top opening seam allowance of the lining bag of Step 3 and insert it into the outer bag of Step 2. Insert the side tabs and handsew a running stitch along the top opening with the Kamogawa thread (B).

5. Attach the zipper pull to the zipper slider.

#04 DUTY-FREE EXPANDABLE CARRY-ALL AND POUCH

No full-size pattern provided.

Cut out the following pieces directly from the fabric:

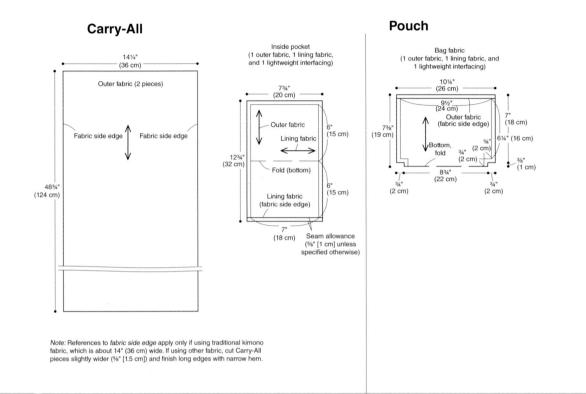

Carry-All

Outer fabric (2 pieces)

14¼" (36 cm)

48¾" (124 cm)

Fabric side edge | Fabric side edge

Inside pocket
(1 outer fabric, 1 lining fabric, and 1 lightweight interfacing)

7¾" (20 cm)

12¾" (32 cm)

Outer fabric

Lining fabric

Fold (bottom)

Lining fabric (fabric side edge)

6" (15 cm)

6" (15 cm)

7" (18 cm)

Seam allowance (⅜" [1 cm] unless specified otherwise)

Pouch

Bag fabric
(1 outer fabric, 1 lining fabric, and 1 lightweight interfacing)

10¼" (26 cm)

9½" (24 cm)

Outer fabric (fabric side edge)

Bottom, fold

7⅜" (19 cm)

7" (18 cm)

6¼" (16 cm)

¾" (2 cm)

¾" (2 cm)

⅜" (1 cm)

8¾" (22 cm)

¾" (2 cm)

¾" (2 cm)

Note: References to fabric side edge apply only if using traditional kimono fabric, which is about 14" (36 cm) wide. If using other fabric, cut Carry-All pieces slightly wider (⅝" [1.5 cm]) and finish long edges with narrow hem.

Carry-All

A

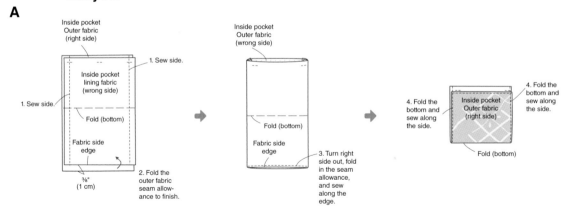

Inside pocket Outer fabric (right side)

1. Sew side.

Inside pocket lining fabric (wrong side)

1. Sew side.

Fold (bottom)

Fabric side edge

⅜" (1 cm)

2. Fold the outer fabric seam allowance to finish.

Inside pocket Outer fabric (wrong side)

Fold (bottom)

Fabric side edge

3. Turn right side out, fold in the seam allowance, and sew along the edge.

4. Fold the bottom and sew along the side.

Inside pocket Outer fabric (right side)

4. Fold the bottom and sew along the side.

Fold (bottom)

B

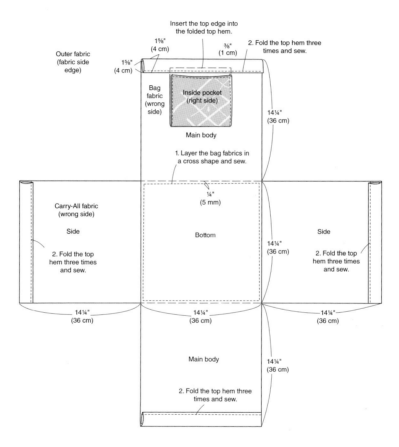

Insert the top edge into the folded top hem.

1⅝" (4 cm)

⅜" (1 cm)

2. Fold the top hem three times and sew.

Outer fabric (fabric side edge)

1⅝" (4 cm)

1⅝" (4 cm)

Bag fabric (wrong side)

Inside pocket (right side)

Main body

14¼" (36 cm)

1. Layer the bag fabrics in a cross shape and sew.

¼" (5 mm)

Carry-All fabric (wrong side)

Side

2. Fold the top hem three times and sew.

Bottom

Side

2. Fold the top hem three times and sew.

14¼" (36 cm)

14¼" (36 cm)

14¼" (36 cm)

14¼" (36 cm)

Main body

2. Fold the top hem three times and sew.

14¼" (36 cm)

#04 DUTY-FREE EXPANDABLE CARRY-ALL AND POUCH

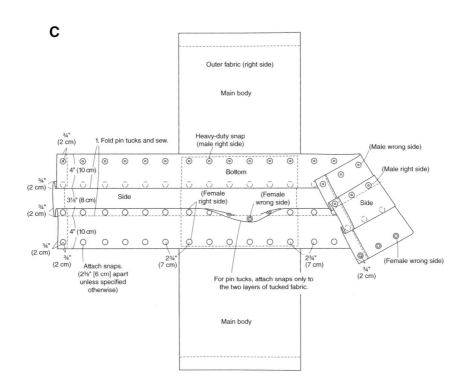

C

Outer fabric (right side)

Main body

¾" (2 cm)

1. Fold pin tucks and sew.

Heavy-duty snap (male right side)

(Male wrong side)

(Male right side)

4" (10 cm)

Bottom

¾" (2 cm)

Side

3⅛" (8 cm)

(Female right side)

(Female wrong side)

Side

¾" (2 cm)

¾" (2 cm)

4" (10 cm)

(Female wrong side)

¾" (2 cm)

¾" (2 cm)

2¾" (7 cm)

2¾" (7 cm)

¾" (2 cm)

Attach snaps. (2⅜" [6 cm] apart unless specified otherwise)

For pin tucks, attach snaps only to the two layers of tucked fabric.

Main body

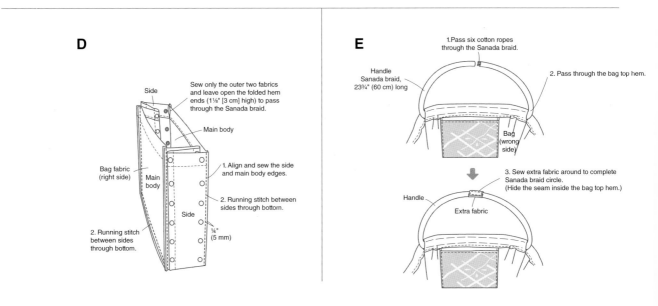

D

Side

Sew only the outer two fabrics and leave open the folded hem ends (1⅛" [3 cm] high) to pass through the Sanada braid.

Main body

Bag fabric (right side)

Main body

1. Align and sew the side and main body edges.

2. Running stitch between sides through bottom.

Side

¼" (5 mm)

2. Running stitch between sides through bottom.

E

1. Pass six cotton ropes through the Sanada braid.

Handle Sanada braid, 23¾" (60 cm) long

2. Pass through the bag top hem.

Bag (wrong side)

3. Sew extra fabric around to complete Sanada braid circle. (Hide the seam inside the bag top hem.)

Handle

Extra fabric

Pouch

A

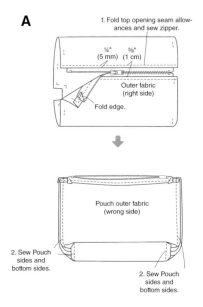

1. Fold top opening seam allowances and sew zipper.

¼"
(5 mm)

⅜"
(1 cm)

Outer fabric
(right side)

Fold edge.

Pouch outer fabric
(wrong side)

2. Sew Pouch
sides and
bottom sides.

2. Sew Pouch
sides and
bottom sides.

B

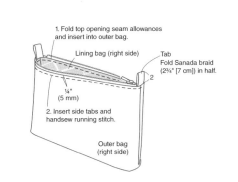

1. Fold top opening seam allowances
and insert into outer bag.

Lining bag (right side)

Tab
Fold Sanada braid
(2¾" [7 cm]) in half.

2

¼"
(5 mm)

2. Insert side tabs and
handsew running stitch.

Outer bag
(right side)

Left Bank Granny Bag and Drawstring Day Bag
COLLECTION #05

Designed with shopping at flea markets and antique fairs in mind, this bag is especially roomy. Its deep side slits allow the bag to open wide, accommodating anything you want to toss in there. Precise measurement is unnecessary when pin tucking the top edge; simply use the fabric's stripe pattern as a guide for a well-balanced finish.

About the Fabric

This unique striped linen print was originally bought with a skirt project in mind. Tightly woven, this fabric has a structure that will wear well over time, even with ample use.

Left Bank Granny Bag

18⅜" × 17" × 5½" (46 × 43 × 14 cm)

Drawstring Day Bag

7⅞" × 9¾" × 1⅝" (20 × 25 × 4 cm)

Materials

Striped linen (outer fabric, top opening rim fabric and handles of the Granny Bag; outer fabric and loops of the Drawstring Bag): 32" × 59" (80 × 150 cm)

Red cotton twill (lining bag fabric and inside pockets): 36" × 44" (90 × 110 cm)

Lightweight fusible interfacing (for outer bag fabric, top opening rim, and handles of the Granny Bag; outer bag fabric and inside pocket of the Drawstring Bag): 40" × 48" (100 × 120 cm)

Zipper (1, for Granny Bag inside pocket): 8" (20 cm)

Leather cord (for Drawstring Bag): ¼" × 48" (5 mm × 122 cm)

Beads (to attach to cords on Drawstring Bag): Two ½" (10 mm) diameter, two ¼" (4–5 mm) diameter

Linen thread (optional)

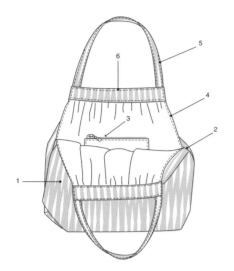

Granny Bag

1. Fuse interfacing to the wrong side of the outer bag fabric pieces, top opening rim fabric pieces, and handles.

2. Fold the outer bag fabric right side in and sew the sides (up to the side opening bottoms) and the bottom corners as shown (A).

3. Sew the inside pocket to the lining bag fabric, inserting the zipper (B). Fold the lining bag fabric right side in and sew the sides (up to the side opening bottoms) and the bottom corners as for outer bag.

4. Insert the lining bag of Step 3 into the outer bag of Step 2 right side in and sew the side seams. Turn right side out, sew along the side opening edges, and pin tuck the top opening as shown (C).

5. Make the handles, sandwich them between the top opening rim fabrics and sew them together (D).

6. Sew the top opening rim fabrics of Step 5 onto the bag of Step 4. Turn the rim fabrics right side out, fold with the bag top sandwiched between, and sew the folded edges (E).

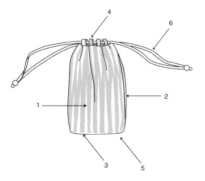

Drawstring Bag

1. Fuse interfacing to the wrong side of the outer bag fabric and inside pocket.

2. Sew the outer bag fabrics right side in along the sides, corners, and bottom (A).

3. Make the inside pocket and sew to the lining bag fabric (see p. 59, B). Sew the lining bag fabrics right side in along the sides, corners, and bottom (leave a small opening for turning).

4. Make the loops and pin to the top opening of the outer bag of Step 2. (B). Insert the lining bag of 3 into the outer bag right side in and sew the top openings together (C).

5. Turn right side out and stitch closed the opening used for turning (D).

6. Press the top opening with the lining bag appearing just above the outer bag top. Pass the leather cord through the loops and attach the beads (E).

#05 LEFT BANK GRANNY BAG AND DRAWSTRING DAY BAG
No full-size pattern provided.

Cut out the following pieces directly from the fabric:

Granny Bag

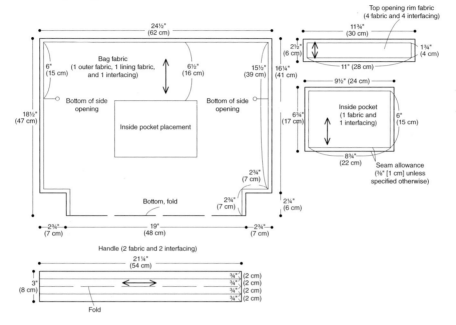

Bag fabric
(1 outer fabric, 1 lining fabric,
and 1 interfacing)

24½" (62 cm)

6" (15 cm)

6½" (16 cm)

15½" (39 cm)

16¼" (41 cm)

18½" (47 cm)

Bottom of side opening

Bottom of side opening

Inside pocket placement

Bottom, fold

2¾" (7 cm)

2¾" (7 cm)

2¼" (6 cm)

2¾" (7 cm)

19" (48 cm)

2¾" (7 cm)

Top opening rim fabric
(4 fabric and 4 interfacing)

11¾" (30 cm)

11" (28 cm)

2½" (6 cm)

1¾" (4 cm)

9½" (24 cm)

Inside pocket
(1 fabric and
1 interfacing)

6¾" (17 cm)

6" (15 cm)

8¾" (22 cm)

Seam allowance
(⅜" [1 cm] unless
specified otherwise)

Handle (2 fabric and 2 interfacing)

21¼" (54 cm)

3" (8 cm)

¾" (2 cm)
¾" (2 cm)
¾" (2 cm)
¾" (2 cm)

Fold

Drawstring Bag

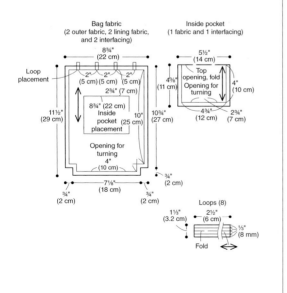

Bag fabric
(2 outer fabric, 2 lining fabric,
and 2 interfacing)

8¾" (22 cm)

Loop placement

2" (5 cm) 2" (5 cm) 2" (5 cm)

2¾" (7 cm)

8¾" (22 cm)
Inside pocket placement

11½" (29 cm)

10" (25 cm)

Opening for turning
4" (10 cm)

7⅛" (18 cm)

¾" (2 cm)

¾" (2 cm)

¾" (2 cm)

Inside pocket
(1 fabric and 1 interfacing)

5½" (14 cm)

Top opening, fold
Opening for turning

4⅜" (11 cm)

4" (10 cm)

4¾" (12 cm)

2¾" (7 cm)

10¾" (27 cm)

Loops (8)

1¼" (3.2 cm)

2½" (6 cm)

⅓" (8 mm)

Fold

A   Granny Bag

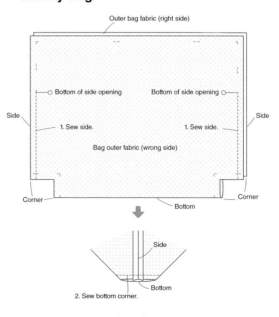

Outer bag fabric (right side)

Bottom of side opening

Bottom of side opening

Side

Side

1. Sew side.

1. Sew side.

Bag outer fabric (wrong side)

Corner

Corner

Bottom

Side

Bottom

2. Sew bottom corner.

B

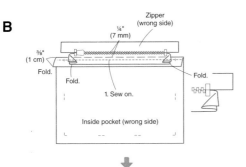

Zipper (wrong side)

¼" (7 mm)

⅜" (1 cm)

Fold.

Fold.

Fold.

1. Sew on.

Inside pocket (wrong side)

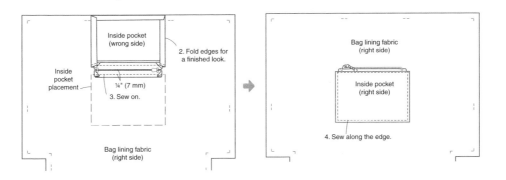

Inside pocket (wrong side)

2. Fold edges for a finished look.

Inside pocket placement

¼" (7 mm)

3. Sew on.

Bag lining fabric (right side)

Bag lining fabric (right side)

Inside pocket (right side)

4. Sew along the edge.

C

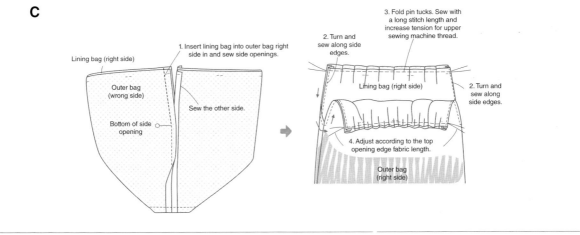

Lining bag (right side)

1. Insert lining bag into outer bag right side in and sew side openings.

Outer bag (wrong side)

Sew the other side.

Bottom of side opening

3. Fold pin tucks. Sew with a long stitch length and increase tension for upper sewing machine thread.

2. Turn and sew along side edges.

Lining bag (right side)

2. Turn and sew along side edges.

4. Adjust according to the top opening edge fabric length.

Outer bag (right side)

D

1. Fold handle widthwise four times and sew along both edges.

Top opening edge fabric (right side)

¾" (2 cm)

2. Sandwich handle and sew top opening edge fabrics right side in.

Top opening edge fabric (wrong side)

Sew to the mark.

Sew up to the mark.

¾" (2 cm)

Handle (right side)

¾" (2 cm)

continued on next page ⊙

#05 LEFT BANK GRANNY BAG AND DRAWSTRING DAY BAG

E

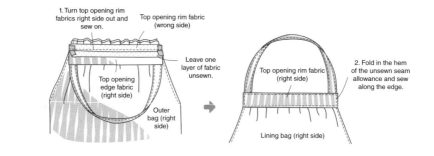

1. Turn top opening rim fabrics right side out and sew on.

Top opening rim fabric (wrong side)

Leave one layer of fabric unsewn.

Top opening edge fabric (right side)

Outer bag (right side)

Top opening rim fabric (right side)

2. Fold in the hem of the unsewn seam allowance and sew along the edge.

Lining bag (right side)

Drawstring Bag

A

Outer bag fabric (wrong side)

Outer bag fabric (right side)

Side

Side

1. Sew sides and bottom.

Corner

Bottom

Corner

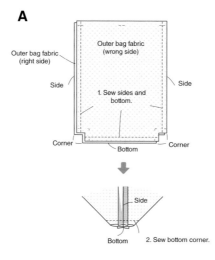

Side

Bottom

2. Sew bottom corner.

B

⅓" (8 mm)

Loop (right side)

1. Fold four times and sew along edge.

2. Pin to outer bag allowance.

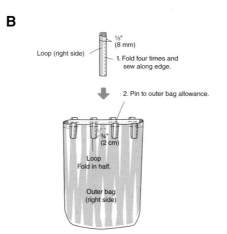

¾" (2 cm)

Loop Fold in half.

Outer bag (right side)

C

Sew.

Lining bag (wrong side)

Outer bag
(wrong side)

D

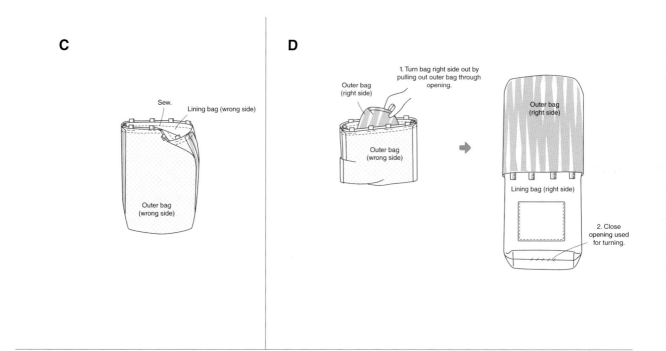

1. Turn bag right side out by
pulling out outer bag through
opening.

Outer bag
(right side)

Outer bag
(wrong side)

Outer bag
(right side)

Lining bag (right side)

2. Close
opening used
for turning.

E

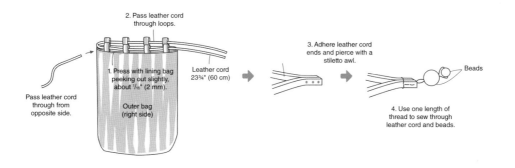

2. Pass leather cord
through loops.

Pass leather cord
through from
opposite side.

1. Press with lining bag
peeking out slightly,
about $\frac{1}{16}$" (2 mm).

Leather cord
23¾" (60 cm)

Outer bag
(right side)

3. Adhere leather cord
ends and pierce with a
stiletto awl.

Beads

4. Use one length of
thread to sew through
leather cord and beads.

Business Class Laptop Bag and Circle Pochette

COLLECTION #06

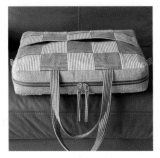

These bags are constructed from a patchwork of three hickory-striped cotton fabrics, alternating vertical and horizontal orientations. The fabrics are easily cut along their stripes lines without requiring precise markings, making it easy for even beginners to create aligned, matching pieces. Try horizontal stripes on the bag depth sections; this way, fabric distortions are camouflaged.

About the Fabric

Cocoa brown and off-white hickory stripes—I must be fond of this color combination since three slightly different versions all made their way into my fabric stash to be used for this Laptop Bag and Circle Pochette. This fabric is sturdy and barely stretches, which makes cutting easy and worrying about the fabric weave direction unnecessary.

Business Class Laptop Bag

15¾" × 12⅝" × 4" (40.5 × 32 × 10 cm)

Circle Pochette

8" diameter × 2" deep (20 × 5 cm)

Materials

Various hickory-striped cottons:

Fabric A (main body outer fabric, handles, tabs, zipper pull, inside pocket top edge fabric of Laptop Bag; side outer fabric of the Pochette): 48" × 24" (120 × 60 cm)

Fabric B (main body outer fabric of Laptop Bag and Pochette): 48" × 16" (120 × 40 cm)

Fabric C (side outer fabric of the Laptop Bag; main body outer fabric, shoulder strap, and zipper pull of the Pochette): 48" × 20" (120 × 50 cm)

Lime green cotton (lining fabric and outer pocket lining fabric of Laptop Bag; inside pocket of Pochette): 48" × 40" (120 × 100 cm)

Lightweight fusible interfacing: 18" × 2½ yd (45 cm × 2.2 m)

2-way zipper (1, for Laptop Bag): 24" (60 cm)

Zipper (1, for Pochette): 12" (30 cm)

Snap (1, for Laptop Bag): ½" (13 mm)

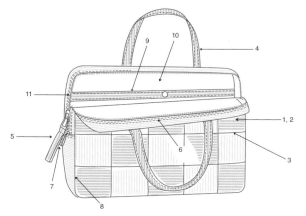

Laptop Bag

1. Fuse interfacing to the wrong side of the outer, lining, and inside pocket fabric pieces. Sew the hickory-striped cottons A and B into alternating patchwork to make the main body outer fabrics. Clip the corners of the main body fabrics according to the diagram (A).

2. Fuse interfacing to the wrong side of the main bodies of Step 1, side outer fabrics, and handles.

3. Sew the front main body outer fabrics and the outer pocket lining fabric (B).

4. Make the handles and pin to the main body outer fabric (C).

5. Make the zipper pulls and attach to the zipper (D).

6. Sew the zipper onto the top side outer fabrics (E).

7. Make the tabs. Sew the top side outer fabric of Step 6 and the bottom side outer fabrics with the tabs sandwiched between, respectively (F).

8. Sew the main body outer fabrics and the side outer fabric of Step 7 right side in.

9. Sew the top edge fabric and the inside pocket and pin to the main body lining fabric. Set the snap (G).

10. Pin the top side and bottom side lining fabrics and sew together with the main body lining fabrics right side in (H).

11. Insert the lining bag of Step 10 into the outer bag of Step 8 and sew lining to zipper tape. Handstitch the unsewn zipper ends (I).

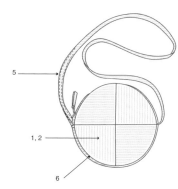

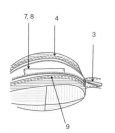

Circle Pochette

1. Sew the hickory-striped cottons B and C into alternating patchwork to make the main body outer fabrics (A).

2. Fuse interfacing to the wrong side of the main bodies of Step 1, side outer fabrics, shoulder strap, and inside pocket.

3. Make the zipper pull and attach it to the zipper (see p. 84, D).

4. Sew the zipper to the top side outer fabrics (B).

5. Make the shoulder strap. Sew the top side outer fabric of Step 4 and the bottom side outer fabrics with the shoulder strap sandwiched between (C).

6. Sew the main body outer fabrics and the side outer fabric of Step 5 right side in.

7. Make the inside pocket and sew to the main body lining fabric (see p. 59, B).

8. Pin the top side and bottom side lining fabrics and sew with the main body lining fabrics right side in (D).

9. Insert the lining bag into the outer bag and sew lining to zipper tape. Handstitch the unsewn zipper ends (E).

#06 BUSINESS CLASS LAPTOP BAG AND CIRCLE POCHETTE

Use Side B for full-size sewing pattern (for Laptop Bag main body, side, outer pocket lining fabric, and inside pocket; and Circle Pochette main body).

Besides the above pattern pieces, cut the following pieces from the fabric:

Laptop Bag

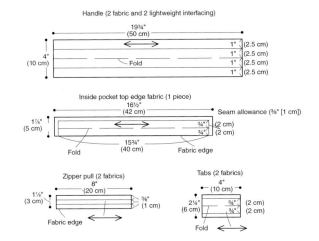

Circle Pochette

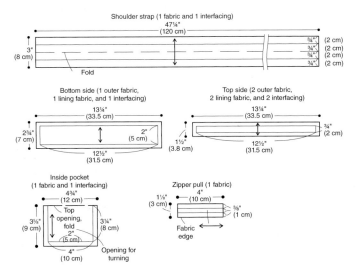

Laptop Bag

A

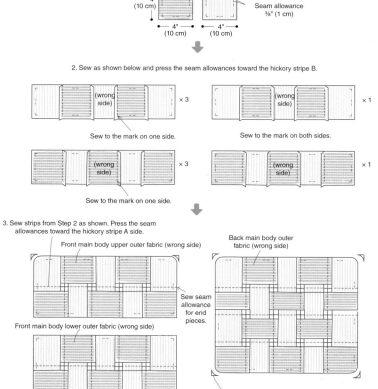

1. Cut squares.

Hickory stripe A
20 squares

Hickory stripe B
20 squares

4" (10 cm)

Seam allowance ⅜" (1 cm)

4" (10 cm)   4" (10 cm)

2. Sew as shown below and press the seam allowances toward the hickory stripe B.

(wrong side) × 3

Sew to the mark on one side.

(wrong side) × 1

Sew to the mark on both sides.

(wrong side) × 3

Sew to the mark on one side.

(wrong side) × 1

3. Sew strips from Step 2 as shown. Press the seam allowances toward the hickory stripe A side.

Front main body upper outer fabric (wrong side)

Back main body outer fabric (wrong side)

Sew seam allowance for end pieces.

Front main body lower outer fabric (wrong side)

4. Clip corners as shown in diagram.

B

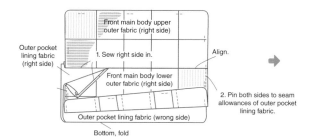

Outer pocket lining fabric (right side)

Front main body upper outer fabric (right side)

1. Sew right side in.

Align.

Front main body lower outer fabric (right side)

2. Pin both sides to seam allowances of outer pocket lining fabric.

Outer pocket lining fabric (wrong side)

Bottom, fold

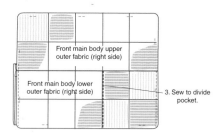

Front main body upper outer fabric (right side)

Front main body lower outer fabric (right side)

3. Sew to divide pocket.

continued on next page ⊙

C

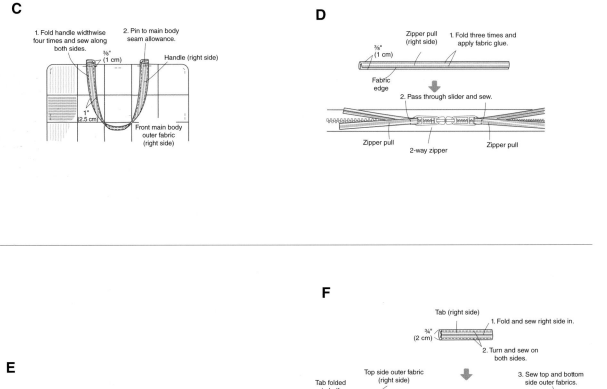

1. Fold handle widthwise four times and sew along both sides.

2. Pin to main body seam allowance.

⅜" (1 cm)

Handle (right side)

1" (2.5 cm)

Front main body outer fabric (right side)

D

Zipper pull (right side)

1. Fold three times and apply fabric glue.

⅜" (1 cm)

Fabric edge

2. Pass through slider and sew.

Zipper pull

2-way zipper

Zipper pull

E

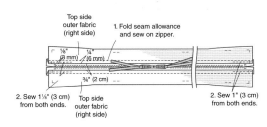

Top side outer fabric (right side)

1. Fold seam allowance and sew on zipper.

⅛" (3 mm) ¼" (6 mm)

¾" (2 cm)

2. Sew 1⅛" (3 cm) from both ends.

Top side outer fabric (right side)

2. Sew 1" (3 cm) from both ends.

F

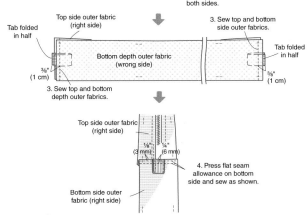

Tab (right side)

1. Fold and sew right side in.

¾" (2 cm)

2. Turn and sew on both sides.

Tab folded in half

Top side outer fabric (right side)

3. Sew top and bottom side outer fabrics.

Bottom depth outer fabric (wrong side)

Tab folded in half

⅜" (1 cm)

⅜" (1 cm)

3. Sew top and bottom depth outer fabrics.

Top side outer fabric (right side)

⅛" (3 mm) ¼" (6 mm)

4. Press flat seam allowance on bottom side and sew as shown.

Bottom side outer fabric (right side)

G

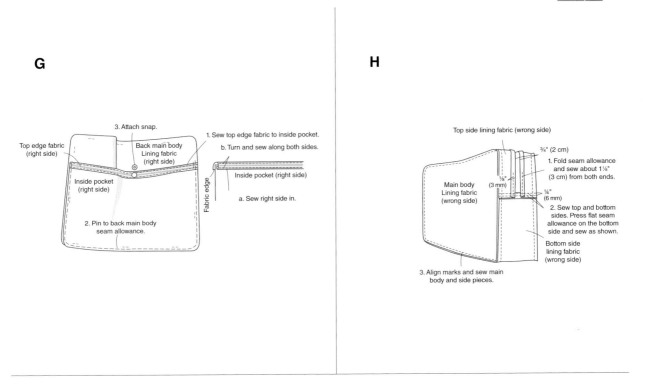

3. Attach snap.

Top edge fabric
(right side)

Back main body
Lining fabric
(right side)

1. Sew top edge fabric to inside pocket.

b. Turn and sew along both sides.

Inside pocket
(right side)

Inside pocket (right side)

Fabric edge

a. Sew right side in.

2. Pin to back main body
seam allowance.

H

Top side lining fabric (wrong side)

¾" (2 cm)

⅛"
(3 mm)

1. Fold seam allowance
and sew about 1⅛"
(3 cm) from both ends.

Main body
Lining fabric
(wrong side)

¼"
(6 mm)

2. Sew top and bottom
sides. Press flat seam
allowance on the bottom
side and sew as shown.

Bottom side
lining fabric
(wrong side)

3. Align marks and sew main
body and side pieces.

I

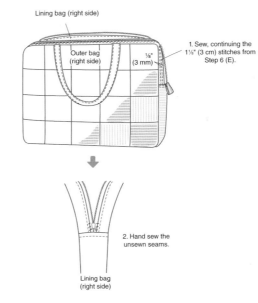

Lining bag (right side)

Outer bag
(right side)

⅛"
(3 mm)

1. Sew, continuing the
1⅛" (3 cm) stitches from
Step 6 (E).

2. Hand sew the
unsewn seams.

Lining bag
(right side)

Circle Pochette

A

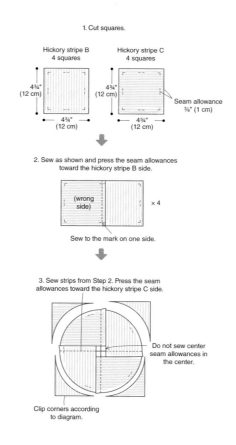

1. Cut squares.

Hickory stripe B
4 squares

Hickory stripe C
4 squares

4¾"
(12 cm)

4¾"
(12 cm)

Seam allowance
⅜" (1 cm)

4¾"
(12 cm)

4¾"
(12 cm)

2. Sew as shown and press the seam allowances
toward the hickory stripe B side.

(wrong side)

× 4

Sew to the mark on one side.

3. Sew strips from Step 2. Press the seam
allowances toward the hickory stripe C side.

Do not sew center
seam allowances in
the center.

Clip corners according
to diagram.

B

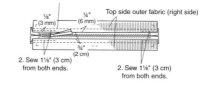

1. Fold seam allowance and insert zipper.

⅛"
(3 mm)

¼"
(6 mm)

Top side outer fabric (right side)

¾"
(2 cm)

2. Sew 1⅛" (3 cm)
from both ends.

2. Sew 1⅛" (3 cm)
from both ends.

C

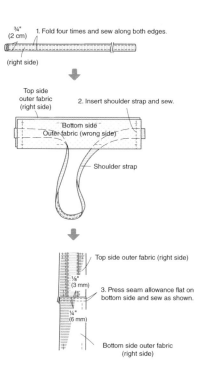

¾"
(2 cm)

1. Fold four times and sew along both edges.

(right side)

Top side
outer fabric
(right side)

2. Insert shoulder strap and sew.

Bottom side
Outer fabric (wrong side)

Shoulder strap

Top side outer fabric (right side)

⅛"
(3 mm)

3. Press seam allowance flat on
bottom side and sew as shown.

¼"
(6 mm)

Bottom side outer fabric
(right side)

D

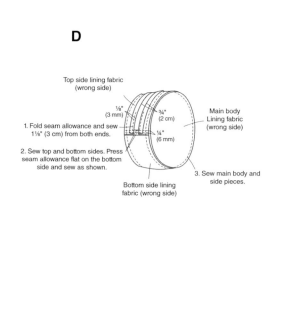

Top side lining fabric
(wrong side)

⅛"
(3 mm)

¾"
(2 cm)

Main body
Lining fabric
(wrong side)

1. Fold seam allowance and sew
1⅛" (3 cm) from both ends.

¼"
(6 mm)

2. Sew top and bottom sides. Press
seam allowance flat on the bottom
side and sew as shown.

Bottom side lining
fabric (wrong side)

3. Sew main body and
side pieces.

E

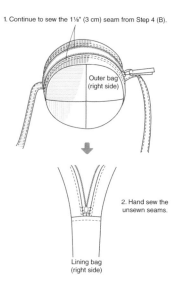

1. Continue to sew the 1⅛" (3 cm) seam from Step 4 (B).

Outer bag
(right side)

2. Hand sew the
unsewn seams.

Lining bag
(right side)

Cabana Tote and Book Cover
COLLECTION #07

The concept of this Cabana Tote emerged from a small piece of multi-colored striped canvas in my stash. The bag was designed to make full use of the fabric, dividing it into two main body panels including the fabric edges. Black canvas (depths and bottom) create vivid contrast with the stripes, and the red leather handles complete the look.

About the Fabric

This multicolor striped canvas from southern France was intended for chair reupholstering. With its thick and tight weave, this fabric is perfect for a sturdy, structured bag. Prewash fabric to remove any creases or folds.

Cabana Tote

15¾" × 13¾" × 6" (40 × 35 × 15 cm)

Book Cover

9½" × 6¼" (24 × 16 cm)

Materials

Multicolor striped canvas fabric (Main body fabric for Cabana Tote and outer fabric for Book Cover)" 18" × 44" (45 × 110 cm)

Black canvas (Side, bottom, small flap cover and inside pocket of Cabana Tote): 36½" × 20" (92 × 50 cm)

Windowpane check or solid-color canvas (lining bag fabric for Cabana Tote): 28" × 40" (70 × 100 cm)

Black lightweight cotton (lining fabric for Book Cover): 16" × 8" (40 × 20 cm)

Heavyweight fusible interfacing (for Cabana Tote bag bottom): 16" × 6" (40 × 15 cm)

Leather strap (for Cabana Tote handles): ¾" × 40" (2 cm × 1 m)

Suede or velvet ribbon (for Book Cover): ⅛" × 10" (4 mm × 25 cm)

Zipper (1, for Cabana Tote): 8" (20 cm)

Twist lock fastener (1 set, for Cabana Tote): ¾" (20 mm)

Bottom rivets (4, for Cabana Tote): ⅜" (10 mm)

Double-sided rivets (8, for Cabana Tote): ⅜" (10 mm)

Snaps (2 sets, for Cabana Tote): ½" (13 mm)

Fabric glue

Rivet setting tool

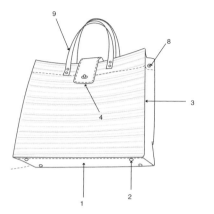

Cabana Tote

1. Fuse interfacing to the wrong side of the bottom fabric. Apply adhesive to the edge along length to wrap the interfacing with the fabric (see p. 108, C).

2. Sew the bag bottom of Step 1 to the two main body panels. Set the bottom rivets (see p. 108, D).

3. Sew the main body-bottom piece of Step 2 to the side fabrics, right side in. Turn bag right side out (A).

4. Make the small flap cover, insert the twist-lock fastener (female piece), and sew onto the back main body of Step 3. Attach the twist-lock fastener (male piece) to the front main body (B).

5. Sew the zipper on the inside pocket. Fold back both sides and sew to make a pocket (C).

6. Sew the main body panels, sides, and bottom of the lining bag fabric.

7. Insert the lining bag of Step 6 into the outer bag. Fold down the outer bag top edge over the lining bag and sew along the hem with the inside pocket of Step 5 sandwiched under folded edge (D).

8. Attach the snaps to the sides (E).

9. Attach the handles with the rivets (F).

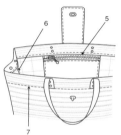

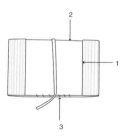

Book Cover

1. Pin the ribbon to the outer fabric. Align the outer and lining fabrics right side in and sew both sides (A).

2. Fold in each side and sew along top and bottom, leaving an opening for turning (B).

3. Turn and blindstitch the bottom opening.

#07 CABANA TOTE AND BOOK COVER

Use Side B for full-size sewing pattern (for small flap cover and side).

Besides the above pattern pieces, cut the following pieces from the fabric:

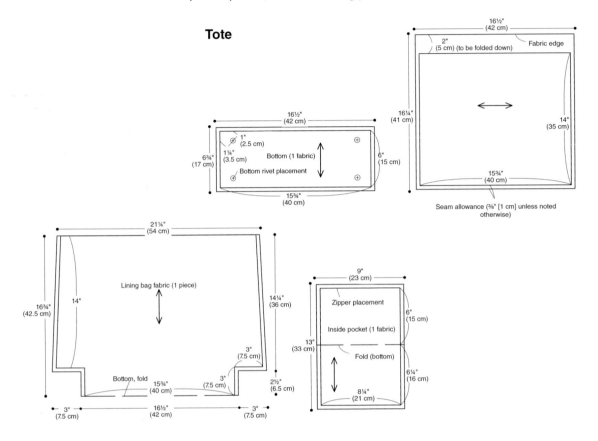

Tote

16½" (42 cm)

1" (2.5 cm)

1¼" (3.5 cm)

Bottom (1 fabric)

Bottom rivet placement

6¾" (17 cm)

6" (15 cm)

15¾" (40 cm)

16½" (42 cm)

2" (5 cm) (to be folded down)

Fabric edge

16¼" (41 cm)

14" (35 cm)

15¾" (40 cm)

Seam allowance (⅜" [1 cm] unless noted otherwise)

21¼" (54 cm)

Lining bag fabric (1 piece)

16¾" (42.5 cm)

14"

14¼" (36 cm)

3" (7.5 cm)

Bottom, fold

15¾" (40 cm)

3" (7.5 cm)

2½" (6.5 cm)

3" (7.5 cm)

16½" (42 cm)

3" (7.5 cm)

9" (23 cm)

Zipper placement

Inside pocket (1 fabric)

6" (15 cm)

13" (33 cm)

Fold (bottom)

6¼" (16 cm)

8¼" (21 cm)

Tote

A

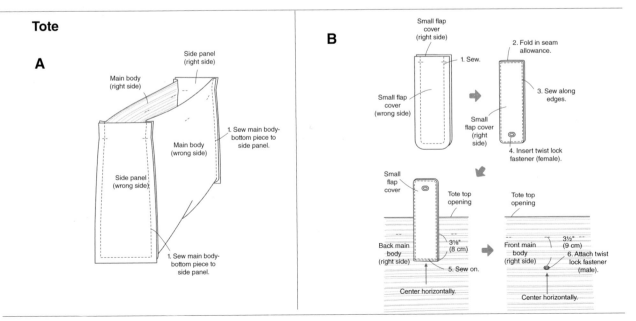

Side panel (right side)

Main body (right side)

1. Sew main body-bottom piece to side panel.

Main body (wrong side)

Side panel (wrong side)

1. Sew main body-bottom piece to side panel.

B

Small flap cover (right side)

1. Sew.

2. Fold in seam allowance.

Small flap cover (wrong side)

3. Sew along edges.

Small flap cover (right side)

4. Insert twist lock fastener (female).

Small flap cover

Tote top opening

Back main body (right side)

3⅛" (8 cm)

5. Sew on.

Center horizontally.

Tote top opening

Front main body (right side)

3½" (9 cm)

6. Attach twist lock fastener (male).

Center horizontally.

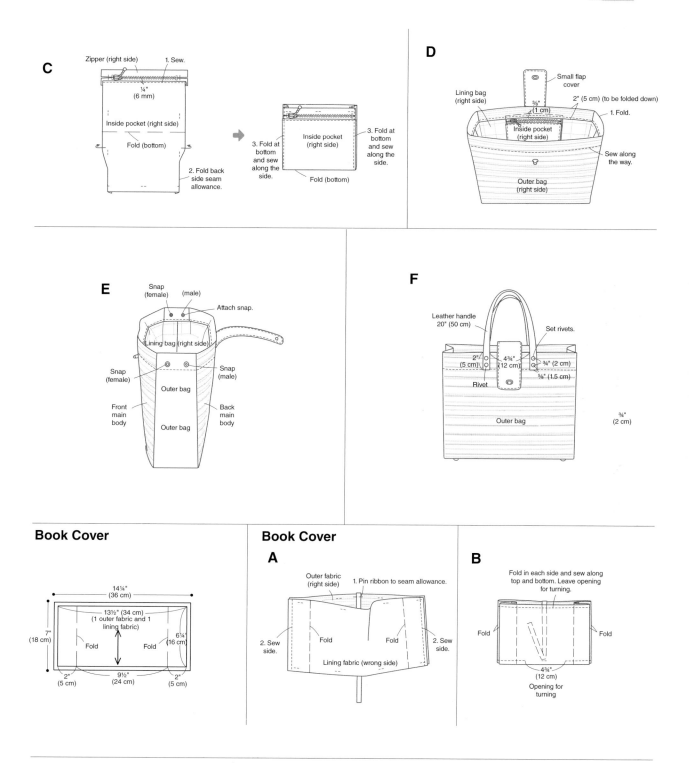

C

Zipper (right side)   1. Sew.

¼"
(6 mm)

Inside pocket (right side)

Fold (bottom)

2. Fold back
side seam
allowance.

3. Fold at
bottom
and sew
along the
side.

Inside pocket
(right side)

3. Fold at
bottom
and sew
along the
side.

Fold (bottom)

D

Small flap
cover

Lining bag
(right side)

2" (5 cm) (to be folded down)

⅜"
(1 cm)

1. Fold.

Inside pocket
(right side)

Sew along
the way.

Outer bag
(right side)

E

Snap
(female)   (male)

Attach snap.

Lining bag (right side)

Snap
(female)

Snap
(male)

Front
main
body

Outer bag

Back
main
body

Outer bag

F

Leather handle
20" (50 cm)

Set rivets.

2"
(5 cm)

4¾"
(12 cm)

¾" (2 cm)

Rivet

⅝" (1.5 cm)

Outer bag

¾"
(2 cm)

Book Cover

14¼"
(36 cm)

13½" (34 cm)
(1 outer fabric and 1
lining fabric)

7"
(18 cm)

6¼"
(16 cm)

Fold   Fold

2"
(5 cm)

9½"
(24 cm)

2"
(5 cm)

Book Cover

A

Outer fabric
(right side)

1. Pin ribbon to seam allowance.

2. Sew
side.

Fold   Fold

2. Sew
side.

Lining fabric (wrong side)

B

Fold in each side and sew along
top and bottom. Leave opening
for turning.

Fold   Fold

4¾"
(12 cm)

Opening for
turning

Sidecar Messenger Bag and Corsage Rosette
COLLECTION #08

Peek beneath the bold purple flap and find a beautiful vintage floral print inside. One of the creative thrills of bag making is to mix and match colors, motifs, and materials. Finding the perfect tortoise shell buckle for this bag was as gratifying as placing the last piece of a jigsaw puzzle.

About the Fabric

The main fabric is plum-colored cotton flannel. The floral lining was found at a Paris flea market; it may have been an interior design remnant.

Sidecar Messenger Bag

14¼" × 10¼" × 3½" (36 × 26 × 9 cm)

Rosette

2" (5 cm)

Materials

Cotton Flannel (outer fabric for front and back panels, side panels, bottom,
   shoulder strap, belt attachment, and bag tassel for Sidecar Messenger Bag;
   flower petals and bottom patch for the Rosette): 60" × 28" (150 × 70 cm)
Rayon print (lining fabric, outer pocket lining fabric, and inside pocket of the
   Sidecar Messenger Bag): 36" × 63" (90 × 160 cm)
Lightweight fusible interfacing (for all outer and lining fabrics except for
   shoulder strap outer fabric, tassel, and Rosette of Sidecar Messenger Bag):
   17¾" × 3 yds (45 cm × 2.7 m)
Heavyweight fusible interfacing (for bottom of Sidecar Messenger Bag):
   12¾" × 3½" (32 × 9 cm)
Zipper (1, for Sidecar Messenger Bag): 8" (20 cm)
Buckle (1, for Sidecar Messenger Bag): 1" (2.4 cm)
Rings (2, for Sidecar Messenger Bag): 1⅛" (3 cm)
Jump ring (1, for Sidecar Messenger Bag): ⅜" (8 mm)
Eye bolt (1, for Sidecar Messenger Bag): ½" (1.2 cm)
Craft wire flower stamens (9, for Rosette): 2½" (6 cm)
Pin back (1, for Rosette): 1⅛" (3 cm)
Fabric glue

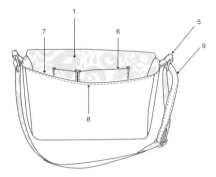

Sidecar Messenger Bag

1. Fuse lightweight interfacing to the wrong side of all outer and lining fabrics except the tassel and the shoulder strap outer fabric. Fuse heavyweight interfacing to the bottom.

2. Make and pin the outer pocket to the back main body/flap cover outer fabric (A).

3. Sew the bottom and side outer fabrics.

4. Sew the piece from Step 3 and outer fabrics of the front main body and the back main body/flap cover (B).

5. Make each strap attachment, pass each through the ring, and pin to the side top seam allowance (C).

6. Make the inside pocket and sew onto the back main body/flap cover lining fabric (see p. 53, B). Sew together with the front main body and side lining fabrics.

7. Insert the lining bag into the outer bag right side in and sew along the top and flap cover edges, leaving an opening for turning (D).

8. Turn right side out and press the top opening.

9. Make the shoulder strap, pass it through the buckle and rings, and sew ends (E).

10. Make the tassel and attach to the outer pocket zipper (F).

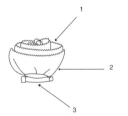

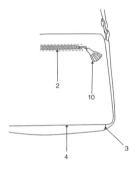

Rosette

1. Cut along one long edge with pinking shears. On the other long edge, round one of the bottom corners. Machine sew with long stitches and a high upper thread tension. Cut thread, then pull the upper thread tail to gather (A).

2. Insert craft flower stamens in the center of the flower, sew to secure them, then arrange the stamens ends into a circle (B).

3. Affix the patch to the bottom with fabric glue and sew on the pin back (C).

#08 SIDECAR MESSENGER BAG AND CORSAGE ROSETTE

Use Side A for full-size sewing pattern (for front main body, back main body/flap cover and side).

Besides the above pattern pieces, cut out the following pieces from the fabric:

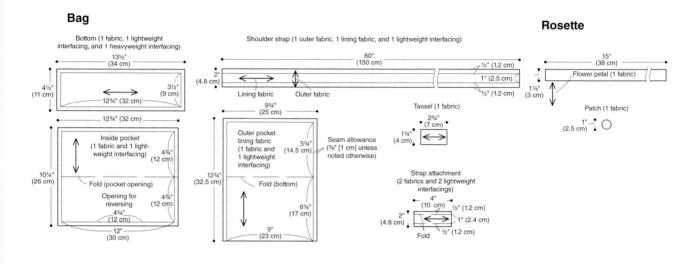

Bag

Bottom (1 fabric, 1 lightweight interfacing, and 1 heavyweight interfacing)

13½" (34 cm)
3½" (9 cm)
4½" (11 cm)
12¾" (32 cm)

12¾" (32 cm)

Inside pocket (1 fabric and 1 lightweight interfacing)
4¾" (12 cm)
10¼" (26 cm)
Fold (pocket opening)
Opening for reversing
4¾" (12 cm)
4¾" (12 cm)
12" (30 cm)

Shoulder strap (1 outer fabric, 1 lining fabric, and 1 lightweight interfacing)

60" (150 cm)
½" (1.2 cm)
2" (4.8 cm)
1" (2.5 cm)
½" (1.2 cm)
Lining fabric   Outer fabric

9¾" (25 cm)

Outer pocket lining fabric (1 fabric and 1 lightweight interfacing)
5¾" (14.5 cm)
Seam allowance (⅜" [1 cm] unless noted otherwise)
12¾" (32.5 cm)
Fold (bottom)
6¾" (17 cm)
9" (23 cm)

Tassel (1 fabric)
2¾" (7 cm)
1¾" (4 cm)

Strap attachment (2 fabrics and 2 lightweight interfacings)
4" (10 cm)
½" (1.2 cm)
2" (4.8 cm)
1" (2.4 cm)
Fold
½" (1.2 cm)

Rosette

15" (38 cm)
Flower petal (1 fabric)
1⅛" (3 cm)

Patch (1 fabric)
1" (2.5 cm)

Bag

A

1. Cut and fold fabric back for a finished zipper opening.

Back main body/flap cover outer fabric (wrong side)

2. Set the zipper with fabric glue onto the seam allowances folded in 1.

Back main body/flap cover outer fabric (right side)

Outer pocket lining fabric (right side)

Back main body/flap cover outer fabric (right side)

3. Place the outer pocket lining fabric over the zipper on wrong side and sew from the right side along the lower side of the zipper opening.

4. Fold the outer pocket lining fabric for a finished look and sew along the remaining three edges of the zipper.

Back main body/flap cover outer fabric (wrong side)

Outer pocket lining fabric (wrong side)   Bottom

Outer pocket lining fabric (wrong side)

5. Sew along both sides of the outer pocket lining fabric while keeping the back main body/flap cover fabric free.

Back main body/flap cover outer fabric (wrong side)

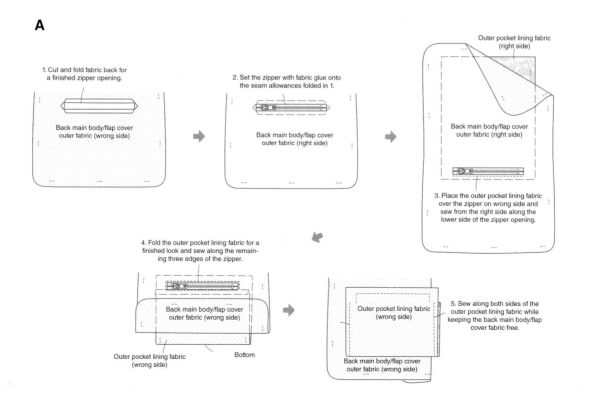

B

Flap cover
outer fabric (right side)

Sew to the mark.

Sew to the mark.

Front main body outer fabric
(wrong side)

Side
Outer fabric
(wrong side)

Match marks and sew
together.

C

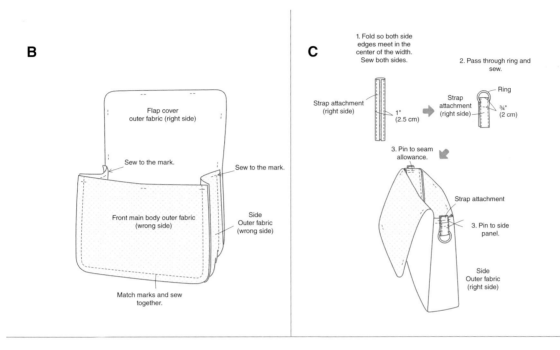

1. Fold so both side
edges meet in the
center of the width.
Sew both sides.

2. Pass through ring and
sew.

Strap attachment
(right side)

1"
(2.5 cm)

Strap
attachment
(right side)

Ring

¾"
(2 cm)

3. Pin to seam
allowance.

Strap attachment

3. Pin to side
panel.

Side
Outer fabric
(right side)

D

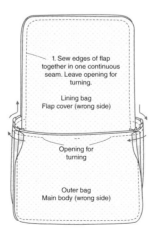

1. Sew edges of flap
together in one continuous
seam. Leave opening for
turning.

Lining bag
Flap cover (wrong side)

Opening for
turning

Outer bag
Main body (wrong side)

continued on next page ▶

#08 SIDECAR MESSENGER BAG AND CORSAGE ROSETTE

E

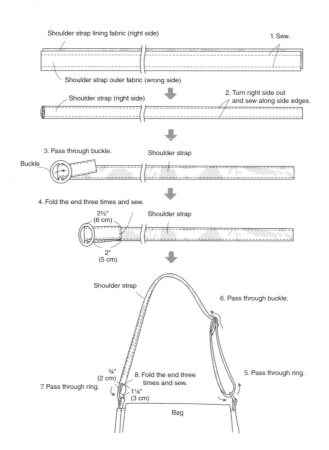

Shoulder strap lining fabric (right side)

1. Sew.

Shoulder strap outer fabric (wrong side)

Shoulder strap (right side)

2. Turn right side out and sew along side edges.

3. Pass through buckle.

Buckle

Shoulder strap

4. Fold the end three times and sew.

2½" (6 cm)

Shoulder strap

2" (5 cm)

Shoulder strap

6. Pass through buckle.

¾" (2 cm)

8. Fold the end three times and sew.

7. Pass through ring.

1⅛" (3 cm)

5. Pass through ring.

Bag

F

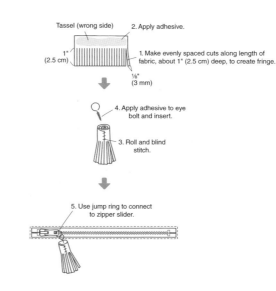

Tassel (wrong side)

2. Apply adhesive.

1" (2.5 cm)

1. Make evenly spaced cuts along length of fabric, about 1" (2.5 cm) deep, to create fringe.

⅛" (3 mm)

4. Apply adhesive to eye bolt and insert.

3. Roll and blind stitch.

5. Use jump ring to connect to zipper slider.

Rosette

A

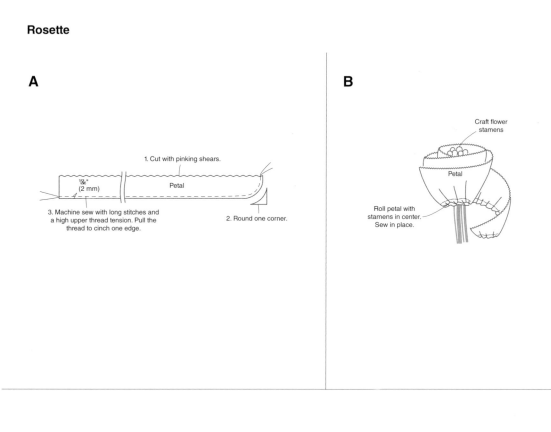

1. Cut with pinking shears.

Petal

$\frac{1}{16}$" (2 mm)

3. Machine sew with long stitches and a high upper thread tension. Pull the thread to cinch one edge.

2. Round one corner.

B

Craft flower stamens

Petal

Roll petal with stamens in center. Sew in place.

C

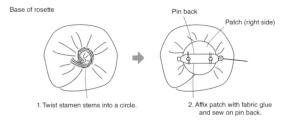

Base of rosette

1. Twist stamen stems into a circle.

Pin back

Patch (right side)

2. Affix patch with fabric glue and sew on pin back.

Market Day Canvas Tote, Azuma Bag, and Furoshiki Wrapping Cloth
COLLECTION #09

Simple and unique, this set incorporates authentic Tenugui Japanese hand towels. Three are used to line the tote, and three make the wrapping cloth (called Furoshiki), which converts to an additional bag when you have light items to carry. The ingenius Azuma Bag is made from just one Tenugui towel or any cotton print fabric.

About the Fabric
The Tenugui Japanese cotton-print hand towels are used whole, without trimming any fabric from the edges. The tote's outer fabric is canvas, ideally high-quality, smooth linen with a sheen.

Market Day Canvas Tote
19" × 15" × 6¼" (48 × 38 × 16 cm)

Azuma Bag
16½" × 6¾" × 3¼" (42 × 17 × 8 cm)

Furoshiki Wrapping Cloth
37¾" × 35½" (96 × 90 cm)

Materials
Natural linen canvas (outer fabric for Market Day Canvas Tote): 37" × 24" (92 × 60 cm)

Tenugui Japanese hand towels (for Market Day Canvas Tote lining fabric): 3 hand towels 13½" × 36" each (34.5 × 91.5 cm each) or cotton print fabric 32" × 37" (81.5 × 94 cm)

Tenugui Japanese hand towel or cotton print (for Azuma Bag): 1 hand towel 13½" × 36" (34.5 × 91.5 cm) or cotton print fabric 13½" × 36" (34.5 × 91.5 cm)

Tenugui Japanese hand towels or cotton print (for Furoshiki Wrapping Cloth): 3 hand towels 13½" × 36" each (34.5 × 91.5 cm each) or cotton print fabric 24" × 37" (61 × 94 cm)

Lightweight fusible interfacing (for lining fabric and inside pocket of the Market Day Canvas Tote): 18" × 55" (45 × 140 cm)

Heavyweight fusible interfacing (for bottom of Market Day Canvas Tote): 12¾" × 6½" (32 × 16 cm)

Leather strap for handles: ¾" wide × 35½" long (2 × 90 cm)

Linen thread, 2 yds (2 m)

Awl for punching holes in leather

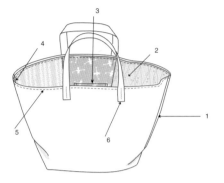

Market Day Canvas Tote

1. Sew the sides and bottom corners of the outer bag fabric (A).

2. Sew together three Japanese hand towels (or cotton print fabrics) and fuse lightweight interfacing to the wrong side. Cut out the lining bag and inside pocket pieces as shown in diagram B.

3. Make the inside pocket and sew onto the lining bag fabric (see p. 59, B). Fuse heavyweight interfacing to wrong side of bottom of bag (C).

4. Sew the sides and bottom corners of the lining bag fabric.

5. Insert the lining bag from Step 4 into the outer bag from Step 1 so wrong sides are together and sew along the top rim (D).

6. Create holes in the leather tape and sew the tape to the outer bag as shown (E).

Azuma Bag

1. Hem short edges of towel or fabric by folding edges down three times; stitch. Mark long edges in thirds and mark with symbols as shown (A).

2. Right sides together, match point A to point B (sides marked with large dot) and stitch seam. Match point C to point D (sides marked with star) and stitch (A).

3. Turn bag right side out as shown (B). Fold triangles to form corners at bottom of bag and stitch. Hem remaining raw edges by folding edges three times and stitching.

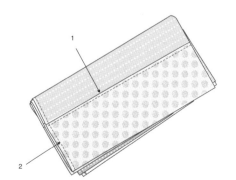

Furoshiki Wrapping Cloth

1. Sew together three Japanese hand towels (or cotton print fabrics) with flat-fell seams as shown in the diagram (A).

2. Fold down each of the upper and lower edges three times and hem (B).

#09 MARKET DAY CANVAS TOTE, AZUMA BAG, AND FUROSHIKI WRAPPING CLOTH

No full-size pattern provided.

Cut out the following pieces from the fabric:

Tote

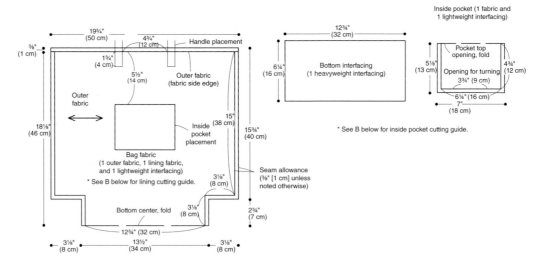

A   Tote

1. Sew sides.

Outer bag fabric (wrong side)

1. Sew sides.

2. Sew bottom corner.

2. Sew bottom corner.

B

Japanese hand towel (or cotton print) (wrong side)

⅜" (1 cm)

6¼" (16 cm)   6¼" (16 cm)   6¼" (16 cm)

1. Cut three Japanese hand towels into 7" (18 cm) sections and sew together.

2. Fuse lightweight interfacing.

3. Cut lining bag shape.

4. Cut inside pocket piece from the extra Japanese hand towel (or cotton print).

Inside pocket

* Sew together small pieces of fabric if the largest extra towel piece is smaller than the size of inside pocket.

C

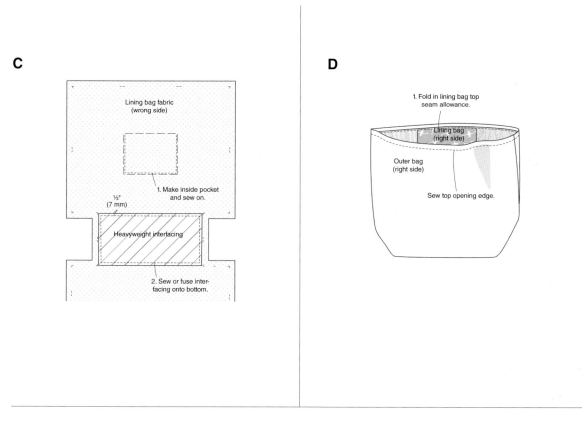

Lining bag fabric
(wrong side)

1. Make inside pocket
and sew on.

½"
(7 mm)

Heavyweight interfacing

2. Sew or fuse inter-
facing onto bottom.

D

1. Fold in lining bag top
seam allowance.

Lining bag
(right side)

Outer bag
(right side)

Sew top opening edge.

E

1. Create 7 holes
with stiletto awl.

2. Stitch handles to bag with large
needle and linen thread at handle
placement marks.

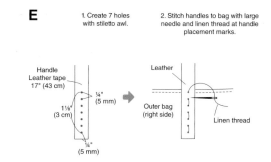

Handle
Leather tape
17" (43 cm)

¼"
(5 mm)

1⅛"
(3 cm)

¼"
(5 mm)

Leather

Outer bag
(right side)

Linen thread

#09 MARKET DAY CANVAS TOTE, AZUMA BAG, AND FUROSHIKI WRAPPING CLOTH

Azuma Bag

A

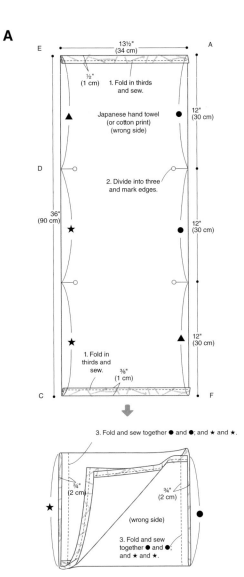

E — 13½" (34 cm) — A

½" (1 cm)

1. Fold in thirds and sew.

▲   Japanese hand towel (or cotton print) (wrong side)   ●   12" (30 cm)

D   ○   ○

2. Divide into three and mark edges.

36" (90 cm)

★   ●   12" (30 cm)

○   ○

★   ▲   12" (30 cm)

1. Fold in thirds and sew.   ⅜" (1 cm)

C — F

3. Fold and sew together ● and ●; and ★ and ★.

¾" (2 cm)   ¾" (2 cm)

★   (wrong side)   ●

3. Fold and sew together ● and ●; and ★ and ★.

B

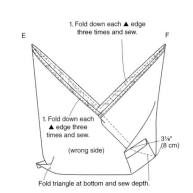

E   1. Fold down each ▲ edge three times and sew.   F

1. Fold down each ▲ edge three times and sew.

(wrong side)   3⅛" (8 cm)

Fold triangle at bottom and sew depth.

Wrapping Cloth

A

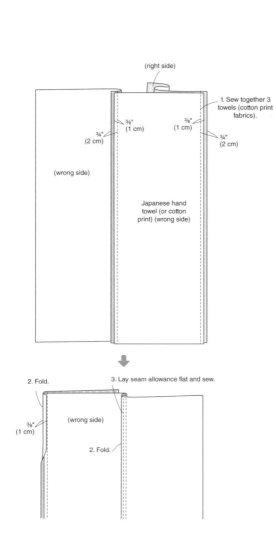

(right side)

1. Sew together 3 towels (cotton print fabrics).

⅜" (1 cm)

⅜" (1 cm)

¾" (2 cm)

¾" (2 cm)

(wrong side)

Japanese hand towel (or cotton print) (wrong side)

2. Fold.

3. Lay seam allowance flat and sew.

(wrong side)

⅜" (1 cm)

2. Fold.

B

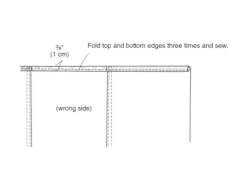

⅜" (1 cm)

Fold top and bottom edges three times and sew.

(wrong side)

Urban Travel Trunk and Luggage Tag
COLLECTION #10

This is a serious bag with seriously detailed construction…with a touch of playful color. Measure carefully, mark precisely, and sew carefully, and you'll reap the benefits after finishing this piece!

About the Fabric

The fabric of choice is waterproof canvas with a paraffin coating, but other water-resistant canvas may be used. Coated canvas may retain folds and creases, but pressing with a warm iron will smooth them out. Camouflage print fabric is used for the lining, adding a touch of irreverence to the design.

Urban Travel Trunk

16½" × 11¾" × 4¾" (42 × 30 × 12 cm)

Luggage Tag

3½" × 1¾" (9 × 4.5 cm)

Materials

Khaki coated canvas (main body, outer pocket, and side outer fabric): 36" × 44" (90 × 110 cm)

Black canvas (bottom outer fabric, handles, straps, loop, piping, and Luggage Tag):
36" × 40" (90 × 100 cm)

Camouflage print or other fabric such as durable canvas or denim (lining fabric, inside pocket, and outer pocket lining fabric): 36" × 48" (90 × 120 cm)

Lightweight fusible interfacing (for lining fabric, small inside pocket, outer pocket lining fabric):
18" × 76" (45 × 190 cm)

Heavyweight fusible interfacing (for Urban Travel Trunk bottom): 4" × 16½" (10 × 42 cm)

Buckles (4): ¾" (2 cm)

Grommets (39): #300 ⅜" (9 mm)

Bottom rivets (4): ⅜" (10 mm)

Two-way zipper (1): 38¼" (97 cm)

Elastic: ¼" wide × 14½" long (5 mm × 37 cm)

Cotton cord (for Urban Travel Trunk piping): 1⁄16" (2 mm) wide × 3⅛ yds (2.8 m)

Jump rings (for Luggage Tag): One ½" (12 mm), one ¾" (21 mm)

Chain (for Luggage Tag): ¼" (5 mm) wide × 2" (5 cm) long

Fabric glue

Grommet hole puncher

Buttonhole chisel

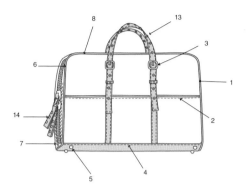

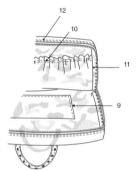

Urban Travel Trunk

1. Fuse lightweight interfacing to the wrong side of the main body, bottom and side lining fabrics, and the small inside pocket fabric.

2. Make the piping and affix it to the outer pocket. Pin the outer pocket to one of the main body outer fabrics (A).

3. Make the straps, create holes in the weave using grommet hole puncher, and pass ends through the buckles. Sew the straps onto the main body outer fabric and attach the belt loops (B).

4. Wrap heavyweight interfacing with the bottom outer fabric seam allowance and affix with fabric glue (C).

5. Sew together the main body outer fabrics from Step 3 and the bottom from Step 4. Set bottom rivets (D).

6. Make more piping and pin it to the main body/bottom outer fabric of Step 5. (E).

7. Sew the zipper onto the side outer fabrics (F).

8. Sew the main body/bottom piece of Step 6 to the side of Step 7, right side in (G).

9. Make the small inside pocket and sew to the main body/bottom lining fabric (see p. 59, B).

10. Make the large inside pocket and sew to the main body/bottom lining fabric (H).

11. Sew the main body/bottom lining pieces to the side lining fabrics, right side in (I).

12. Insert the lining bag of Step 11 into the outer bag of Step 8 and sew lining to zipper tape (J). Handstitch the unsewn zipper ends (see p. 85, I).

13. Make the handles and set the grommets (K).

14. Make the zipper pulls, attach to the zipper sliders, and set the grommets (L).

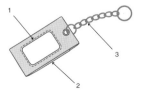

Luggage Tag

1. Make the tag window (A).

2. Fold fabric in thirds, right side in. Sew top and bottom edges and turn right side out (B).

3. Set the grommet, jump rings, and chain (C).

#10 URBAN TRAVEL TRUNK AND LUGGAGE TAG

Use Side B for full-size sewing pattern (for main body, main body/bottom, large inside pocket, and Luggage Tag).

Besides the above pattern pieces, cut the following pieces from the fabric:

Trunk

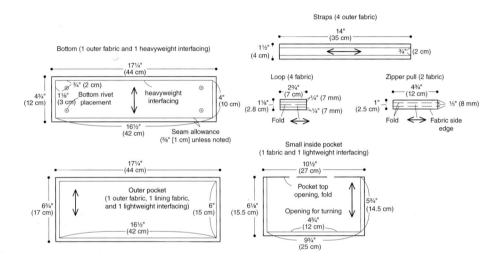

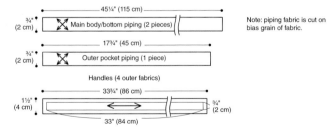

Note: piping fabric is cut on bias grain of fabric.

Trunk

A

B

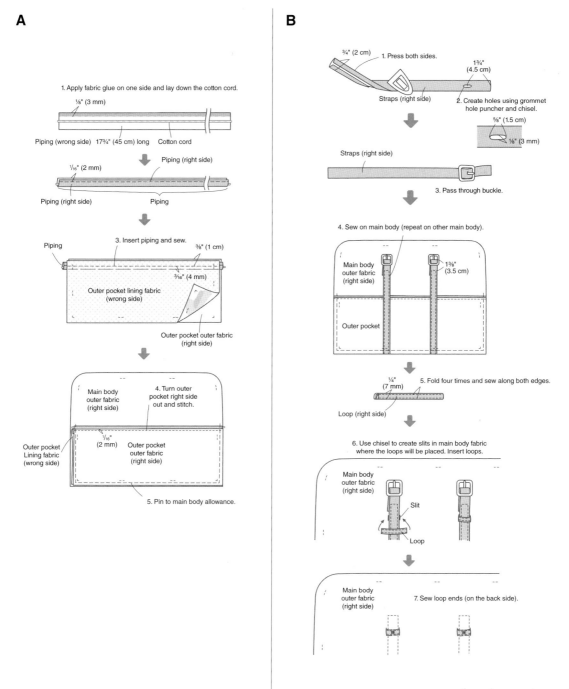

continued on next page ⊙

C

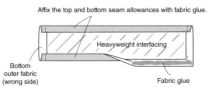

Affix the top and bottom seam allowances with fabric glue.

Heavyweight interfacing

Bottom outer fabric (wrong side)

Fabric glue

D

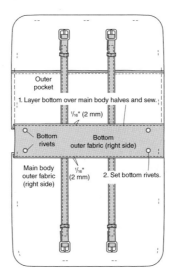

Outer pocket

1. Layer bottom over main body halves and sew.

$^{1}/_{16}$" (2 mm)

Bottom rivets

Bottom outer fabric (right side)

Main body outer fabric (right side)

$^{1}/_{16}$" (2 mm)

2. Set bottom rivets.

E

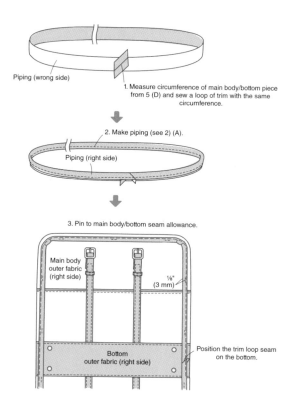

Piping (wrong side)

1. Measure circumference of main body/bottom piece from 5 (D) and sew a loop of trim with the same circumference.

2. Make piping (see 2) (A).

Piping (right side)

3. Pin to main body/bottom seam allowance.

Main body outer fabric (right side)

⅛" (3 mm)

Bottom outer fabric (right side)

Position the trim loop seam on the bottom.

F

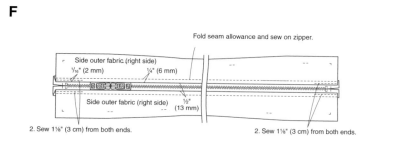

Fold seam allowance and sew on zipper.

Side outer fabric (right side)

1/16" (2 mm)   ¼" (6 mm)

Side outer fabric (right side)   ½" (13 mm)

2. Sew 1⅛" (3 cm) from both ends.

2. Sew 1⅛" (3 cm) from both ends.

#10 URBAN TRAVEL TRUNK AND LUGGAGE TAG

G

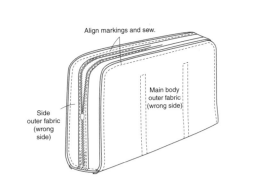

Align markings and sew.

Main body outer fabric (wrong side)

Side outer fabric (wrong side)

H

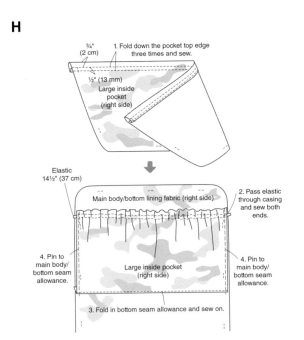

¾" (2 cm)

1. Fold down the pocket top edge three times and sew.

½" (13 mm)

Large inside pocket (right side)

Elastic 14½" (37 cm)

Main body/bottom lining fabric (right side)

2. Pass elastic through casing and sew both ends.

4. Pin to main body/ bottom seam allowance.

Large inside pocket (right side)

4. Pin to main body/ bottom seam allowance.

3. Fold in bottom seam allowance and sew on.

I

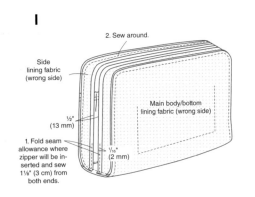

2. Sew around.

Side lining fabric (wrong side)

Main body/bottom lining fabric (wrong side)

½" (13 mm)

1/16" (2 mm)

1. Fold seam allowance where zipper will be inserted and sew 1⅛" (3 cm) from both ends.

J

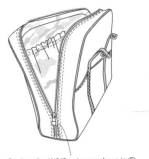

Continue the 1⅛" (3 cm) seam shown in (F).

K

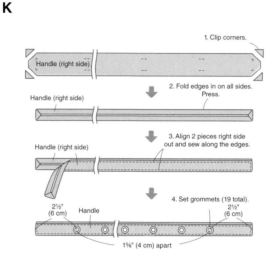

1. Clip corners.

Handle (right side)

2. Fold edges in on all sides. Press.

Handle (right side)

3. Align 2 pieces right side out and sew along the edges.

Handle (right side)

4. Set grommets (19 total).

2½" (6 cm)   Handle   2½" (6 cm)

1⅝" (4 cm) apart

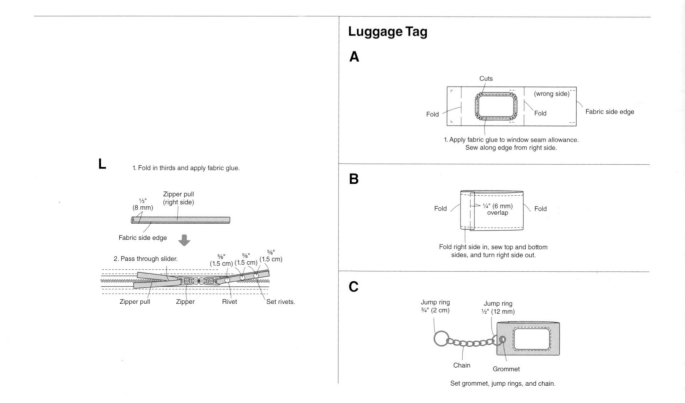

L

1. Fold in thirds and apply fabric glue.

⅓" (8 mm)

Zipper pull (right side)

Fabric side edge

2. Pass through slider.

⅝" (1.5 cm)   ⅝" (1.5 cm)   ⅝" (1.5 cm)

Zipper pull   Zipper   Rivet   Set rivets.

Luggage Tag

A

Cuts

Fold   (wrong side)   Fold   Fabric side edge

1. Apply fabric glue to window seam allowance. Sew along edge from right side.

B

Fold   ¼" (6 mm) overlap   Fold

Fold right side in, sew top and bottom sides, and turn right side out.

C

Jump ring ¾" (2 cm)   Jump ring ½" (12 mm)

Chain   Grommet

Set grommet, jump rings, and chain.

Resources

Handbag Findings and Hardware

Beacon Fabric & Notions
beaconfabric.com
Canvas and cotton duck, interfacing, grommets, zippers and zipper pulls, swivel hooks, and other handbag hardware

Homestead Heirlooms
homesteadheirlooms.com
The "Leather Ladies" specialize in leather straps for bag crafters

Newark Dressmaker Supply
newarkdress.com
Handbag supplies, including purse frames, purse feet, and swivel hooks

Tall Poppy Craft
tallpoppycraft.com
Rivets, twist locks, purse feet, purse frames, and more

U-Handbag
u-handbag.com
Handbag-making supplies for the home sewist

Traditional Japanese Fabrics

Ah! Kimono
ahkimono.com
Vintage kimono fabrics

Bohemian Element
bohemianelement.com
Kasuri cloth (Japanese cotton indigo-dyed handwoven ikat fabric, 14" wide)

Fabric Indulgence and Art Supply
fabricandart.com
Japanese cotton prints and dobby weaves, sashiko fabrics, and yuzen fabrics

Katie's Vintage Kimono
katiesvintagekimono.com
Vintage kimono fabrics

Kimono Lily
kimonolily.com
Vintage kimono fabrics

Wuhao NYC
wuhaonyc.com
Tenugui towels

Contemporary Japanese Fabrics

Purl Soho
purlsoho.com
Japanese cottons and linens

Reprodepot Fabrics
reprodepot.com
Japanese cottons and linens

Superbuzzy
superbuzzy.com
Contemporary Japanese fabric and crafting supplies